REVOLUTION

A BIBLE STUDY FOR TEENAGERS

The BlueFish TV Network Presents *REVOLUTION*

Marty Mosley: Publisher
Randy Petersen: Writer
Jackie Mosley: Editor
J.D. Busch: Art Director/Designer

Published by the BlueFish TV Network

Printed in the U.S.A.

Contents

Articles

Lessons

AN UPRISING

Marty and Jackie Mosley

There is a **Revolution** going on. And you, as a youth worker are right in the middle of the uprising. Teens today are struggling against the culture, against stereotypes, against their unpredictable emotions to find their identity in Christ. You have taken on quite an awesome task to guide your students on their spiritual journey.

To help you, we've created *Revolution*, 13 weeks of curriculum that can easily integrate into your Sunday morning Bible study, a home Bible study group, or other group weekends or retreats.

We are excited to be working again with Doug Fields from Saddleback Church and author of "Purpose Driven Youth Ministry." With over 25 years of experience, Doug continues to amaze at his passion for youth and his talent for helping youth workers. We know your group will love the real-life stories from teens and Doug's practical and Biblical teaching.

The two weeks before you begin using *Revolution*, show your group the fast-paced, emotionally-charged two minute trailer found at the beginning of Show One: *Guilt*. This will set the stage for the whole series.

Make sure each week to go online to BlueFishTV.com and download student handouts for each lesson in the Leader's Guide. And stick around to browse around our site to see other cutting-edge material for youth.

Keep in touch. It is encouraging to hear how your students are growing in Christ.

Blessings,

Jackie Mosley

Jackie Mosley
Producer, *Revolution*

CARING FOR ANGRY PARENTS in your youth group

by Doug Fields

Within every youth ministry, you will find angry parents—angry for good reasons and bad. How you respond to them determines whether you gain credibility or lose respect. Don't try to avoid conflicts or pray that issues will be resolved in silence; they won't. I'm not expecting you to enjoy conflict. I am offering four ideas to help you resolve conflict in your parent and youth worker relationships.

1. DON'T AVOID ANGRY PARENTS.

Angry parents typically call at the peak of their frustration, when they're likely to express themselves with more emotion than reason. Many times I've been glad I was gone when the call came. If I'm in the office, I'll take the call, but invariably the message to call back buys some time. If possible, instead of calling, make a personal visit. In face-to-face communication, you can read nonverbal communication that isn't recognizable over the phone.

2. LISTEN UNTIL THEY FINISH.

Good communication requires you to allow parents to fully share their feelings without interrupting. It's natural to want to interrupt and clarify their statement; however, once parents have voiced their opinions, you'll have your turn. If the conversation is taking place by phone, take notes and wait until the parent is finished.

3. THINK RATIONALLY, NOT PERSONALLY.

When parents are angry, they might express themselves inappropriately. You might hear a comment like, "You're not qualified to be a youth leader," when what's driving the comment is, "I don't know how to reach my son, and I'm afraid for his future. I go to this church, tithe, and I need your help, but I'm too insecure to admit this." Or "Your trips always cost too much." This may mean, "Money is tight right now, and I could really use some help." Your job is to discern the real issue if it's hidden. Ask God for his wisdom and discernment, before you make contact, if possible.

4. END ON A POSITIVE NOTE.

Ending with positive comments does not mean you give into the whining parent. Concluding in a positive way communicates that you want to pursue peace. I try to allow parents to leave our conversations feeling as though—

- They were heard and understood.
- We've taken steps to resolve the conflict.
- Their input is appreciated. (This is essential to leave the door open for future communication.)
- I've said "I'm sorry. Please forgive me," when necessary. If you've messed up, apologize and ask for forgiveness. Reconcile. You're modeling humility, and humility diffuses anger.

Some conflict creates such turmoil within your soul that you'll feel it in your body. It's difficult to not take criticism personally when you care deeply about what you're doing. You can't avoid conflict. Parents will express their anger in some way. Be prepared, pray, and digest the material in the next chapter on conflict. Learn to face conflict directly because, over time, you'll hone the skills needed for dealing with people. As your skills improve, the situations become easier.

WHEN YOU'RE ANGRY WITH PARENTS.

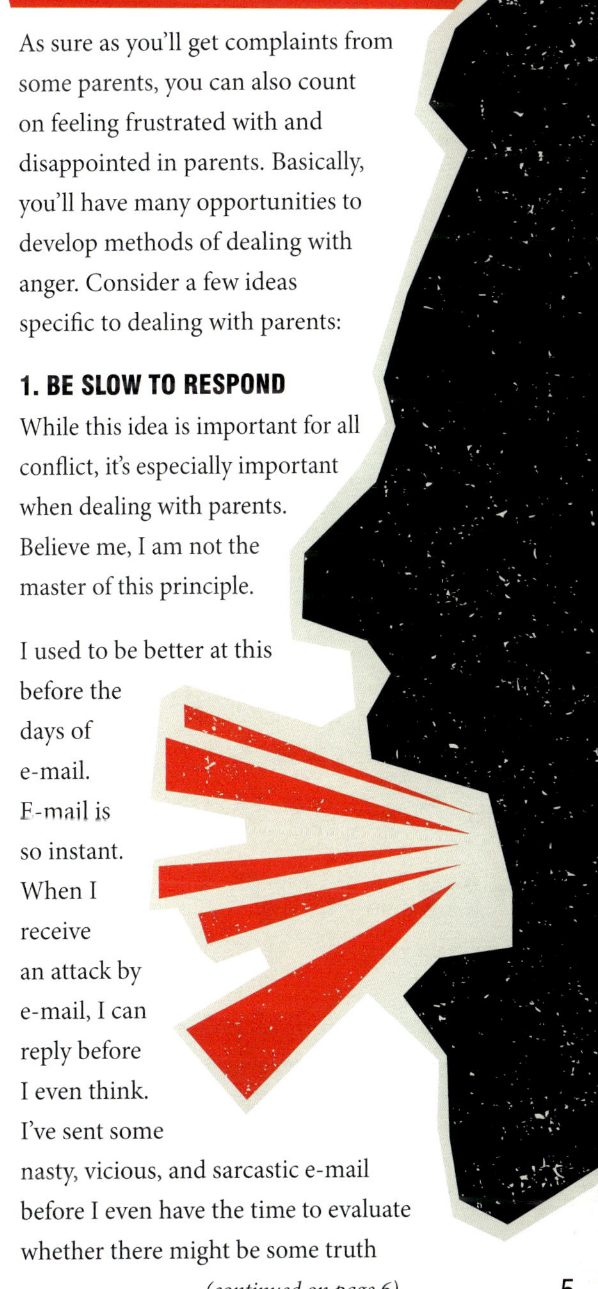

As sure as you'll get complaints from some parents, you can also count on feeling frustrated with and disappointed in parents. Basically, you'll have many opportunities to develop methods of dealing with anger. Consider a few ideas specific to dealing with parents:

1. BE SLOW TO RESPOND

While this idea is important for all conflict, it's especially important when dealing with parents. Believe me, I am not the master of this principle.

I used to be better at this before the days of e-mail. E-mail is so instant. When I receive an attack by e-mail, I can reply before I even think. I've sent some nasty, vicious, and sarcastic e-mail before I even have the time to evaluate whether there might be some truth

(continued on page 6)

> **"We already have too many sitcoms making parents look foolish. We don't need youth workers promoting the stereotype"**

to the message. I regret it every time. I've got to pause, pray, think, ask questions, share my thoughts and feelings with a neutral person, run a marathon, and then wait until I'm rational and less defensive. A good rule is to wait at least 24 hours and allow someone else to read the response before you send it (if you choose to write back at all) to make sure you respond in an appropriate and godly way. You won't lose when you take your time responding.

2. DON'T UNDERMINE PARENTS.

When you're angry with a parent or group of parents, don't try to get their kids on your side. Do not put students in the middle! If students aren't part of the solution, keep them out of the situation.

Take the godly route and steer clear of comments that undermine parents. Parents struggle to keep their children's respect, and you don't help their cause when you demean parents. We already have too many sitcoms making parents look foolish. We don't need youth workers promoting the stereotype – even when it might be true.

3. GO TO THE SOURCE.

I've always lost the battle and damaged my reputation when I've tried to resolve conflicts with parents through third parties (their kids, their spouses, the prayer team, other pastors.) Most conflicts are misunderstandings blown out of proportion by overactive imaginations. When you experience a conflict with parents, go to the parents! Even if the parents don't take this approach, you need to take the higher road and deal with the parent face to face.

4. WALK IN THEIR SHOES.

Many problems happen behind closed doors. You'll never see them. It took several years, but I finally learned this simple principle: there are two sides to every story. When I think like a parent, I understand why parents react the way they do to family conflict. Especially if you're not a parent, put yourself in their shoes and imagine the situation from their perspective. Parents are not the enemies of a healthy youth ministry; they're your greatest allies. ■

Excerpt from "Your First Two Years in Youth Ministry" Copyright 2002 by Doug Fields. Zondervan Publishing House. Order online: ***www.bluefishtv.com***

Doug Fields has been a pastor to students for over 25 years and at Saddleback Church since 1992. His formal education includes a BA from Vanguard University, and a Masters from Fuller Seminary. He is the author of more than 30 books, and the President of Simply Youth Ministry (www.simplyyouthministry.com). His passion for life is time spent with his wife, Cathy, and children Torie, Cody and Cassie.

Objectives

- Group members will learn from the video about guilt feelings and true guilt, their effect on people's lives, and what we can do about them.
- In the lesson, they will be prompted to consider their own guilt feelings (or lack thereof) and how to make things right with God.

Bible Reference

Psalms 103:12; Proverbs 27:17; Matthew 5:23-24; 6:12; Luke 3:8-14; 2 Corinthians 1:12; 1 Timothy 1:4; Hebrews 10:22; 13:18; James 5:16; 1 John 1:9.

Preparation

Go to www.BlueFishTV.com/Handouts and click Revolution Volume 1. Then click on the *Guilt* lesson to download "*Reality Shows*" handout and make copies for the whole class; set up TV/DVD player; *Guilt* DVD; pens/pencils.

Startup

Do you ever watch any of those courtroom shows? Which one?

Do you like them or not? Why or why not?

You have your dramas, like *Law and Order*, and your "reality shows," like *Judge Judy*. Which style do you like the best?

Are you pretty good at figuring out who's guilty on those shows, or not?

That's our subject today: Guilt. It's one thing to watch it on TV, and another when it's something you feel inside. Let's watch.

Showtime

Show *Guilt* video

Re:view

Doug Fields said that when you feel guilty about something, you should remember the G in Guilt. Why? (You should GO to God and to someone else with the issue you're feeling guilty about.)

As Doug put it, there are two people you need to "GO" to. Who? (God and someone else.)

Why is it so important to be accountable to another person? Why can't you just confess things to God and be done with it? (As a spiritual matter, confession to God is sufficient. He forgives the personal, private sins that often cause us guilt. But as a practical matter, it helps us when another human being is checking on us. We can come to take God's forgiveness for granted, but we know a friend will give us a hard time if we mess up again, or at least we'd be embarrassed to fail again.)

Somebody turn to James 5:16. Read that please.

What other things go along with the confession of our sins to one another? (Prayer, healing.)

The Bible also says that we sharpen one another "as iron sharpens iron" (Proverbs 27:17). We help one another find healing and forgiveness and strength against temptation. So if you're feeling guilty about something private, don't keep it to yourself. GO! Go to God and offer it to him, but also find some helpful Christian who might hold you accountable for your actions.

Remember Samuel, who had gotten into pornography, or Courtney, who was dealing with bulimia? If you could talk to either of them, what would you say to them about their guilt feelings? (Both of them are dealing with powerful forces. It's understandable that they feel guilty and ashamed about their actions, but there is hope. God offers forgiveness and freedom, and both of these are important. There are some bad choices they have made. They feel guilty about these, and they should, but God will forgive these sins. Beyond that, there are psychological and emotional issues involved, issues that make it easier to make bad choices. They need to find freedom from these issues, and that may involve counseling.)

At one point, Doug Fields said, "Guilt is a good thing in the life of a Christian." Why would he say that? (Guilt is the alarm that tells us when something is morally wrong with our behavior. If the guilt-alarm is functioning properly, it will alert us when we're going astray from the path God wants for us. We can set things right before things get too bad.)

Imagine a car going down a highway late at night. The driver's beginning to get sleepy, and so the car begins to wander off to the right. If that continues, this could be very dangerous for everything in that car. But on some highways, they have "rumble strips." There's a strip of the roadway outside the main lanes where the pavement is rough. When the car drifts over this rough pavement, what happens? The car rumbles. That wakes everybody up, especially the driver, who can then steer a straight course. Guilt is your moral rumble strip.

Now back to the video. Do you remember Elizabeth, the girl who went drinking and partying instead of going on the mission trip? I'm going to repeat three statements she made and ask for your reaction. I don't do this to pick on her, but there are some important points you might have to deal with.

She said, "Building your relationship with God takes a long time and you don't see immediate results, but whenever you drink you are happy instantly." What do you think? Is that true? (It's sort of true. That's why all sorts of temptations are so tempting to us. They are easy answers. They promise quick happiness, without all the effort of building a relationship with God. Now maybe that "happiness" isn't always so happy. Puking your guts out, doing things you regret later – that's the downside. But Elizabeth is rather astute to point out this comparison. The temptation to drink – or have sex or lie or steal or binge-purge – promises instant happiness, while building a relationship with God takes time.)

She also said, "Like, I believe that God can forgive you for anything." Is that true? (Yes, it's true. God's forgiveness is full and free. We keep trying to put conditions on it, but he doesn't. We keep thinking that he'll forgive you once or twice or seven times, but he promises to keep forgiving us when we ask. The problem is, sometimes we stop asking. We can get so used to sinning that we disable the guilt-alarm and we stop asking God to forgive. That's a dangerous place to be.)

She said, "I decided to . . . get partying out of my system before I went to college." What do you think about that? Was that a good idea? (No! The Big Lie of temptation is thinking that the best way to get rid of temptation is to give in to it. It doesn't work that way. The temptation just gets stronger. It doesn't "get it out of your system," it just puts it deeper within your system.)

Doug Fields talked about driving a car down a rough road. You can get through, but it does damage to your car. Did you get that? What was he trying to say? (You can ignore warning signs and ride over rough road and survive, but it does damage. In the same way, you can continue to ignore God's warnings and eventually get forgiveness for your sin, but those sins do damage to your soul and maybe physical damage too.)

What about Seth who felt guilty about his brother dying in the car crash? Or Ashley, whose mom committed suicide? If you could talk with either of them, what would you say? (These are cases of false guilt. Perhaps there are other emotions that seem like guilt. Certainly there is remorse, there is regret. They wish that they had done things differently or said things differently. But they are not to blame for the tragedies that happened.)

In this video, they talked about true guilt and false guilt. What's the difference? (True guilt is a gift from God. It's a well-functioning moral alarm. It's the voice of the Holy Spirit and your God-given conscience showing you that something is wrong. True guilt doesn't hang around. It needs to be dealt with. You need to confess your sin, repent of it, and seek accountability with others. False guilt is the kind that just sits there. You feel bad about everything; you feel unworthy. It's an over-sensitive conscience rather than the Holy Spirit. Sometimes it's the result of a parent or teacher scolding you too much. The best thing with false guilt is to face up to it. Stare it in the face and sort it out. Maybe there's some true guilt buried within it. Okay, then deal with that. Don't let it be vague. Pin it down. Get specific. What exactly have you done and how wrong is that? Confess what you need to confess and shrug off the rest.)

Just Do It

Leader's Note *Distribute the "Reality Shows" handout.*

As you see on this handout, there are four different situations with guilt feelings and "guilt reality." You may feel guilty because you are guilty, or you may feel guilt-free because you've confessed your sins and received God's forgiveness. In the video today, we saw some of Case 2 and Case 3, where people should have felt guilty but didn't or they felt guilty when they really didn't need to.

What's your situation? Is there a sin you feel bad about and you need to confess it? Then you fit into Case 1. Look over that checklist. Which of those things do you need to do? Whatever needs doing, write it down as your "action step," and be specific.

Maybe you've gotten into some sin. Maybe you're hiding it from others, and you're trying to hide it from God. A long time ago, God made you feel guilty but you've turned off that alarm. Now it's just a little buzz in the back of your brain. Every so often you feel bad that you're not living the good life you're pretending to live, but you still haven't done much about it. Well, that's Case 2. Here are some questions for you. You need to think about the kind of life you want, and what price you're paying for your activity. More than anything, you need to hear God's voice.

Then again, maybe you're the opposite. You have overwhelming feelings of guilt, but you can't get rid of them. The truth may be that you're not really guilty. Or you're not as guilty as you think you are. The best thing to do is to sort through your feelings. What exactly are you feeling guilty for? List those things. Be as specific as possible. Then go through your list and evaluate what step might be required. Notice the Key at the bottom of that part. Do you need to confess this to God and receive his forgiveness? Do you need to get things right with another person? Do you just need to grieve – crying about something, punching a pillow, just being miserable for a few days before you're done with it? Or are there things that you have to say are not your fault. Take a few minutes to sort through those things.

And maybe you're feeling guilt-free because you really are. Not that you never sin. We all sin. But when we sin, we have a Savior who pays for that sin and wins our forgiveness. We can live in his grace, trying to please him more and more.

Pick the case that applies to you and start working through that section. I'm going to give you the next few minutes to do that privately. You can also take it home and work on it there.

Objectives

- Group members will learn from various Scriptures about guilt, sin, sacrifice, and atonement.
- They will consider how God brings about atonement for their own sins.

Bible Reference

Genesis 2-3; Leviticus 6:1-7; 16:7-10; Isaiah 1:11-18; Hebrews 10:19-22.

Preparation

Go to www.BlueFishTV.com/Handouts and click Revolution Volume 1. Then click on the *Blame Game* lesson to download "*Guilty as Sin*" handout and make copies for the whole class; a "thing to throw" for the opening activity (see below); pens/pencils.

Startup

Leader's Note

Line up five potential Culprits and pick one Victim. The Victim stands 8-10 feet from the others, with his or her back turned to them. Announce that a "crime" will be committed and investigated, but the group is to keep silent about it. Then give one of the Culprits something to throw at the back of the victim – a wad of paper, a beanbag, a tomato, a water balloon, depending how messy you want to get.

[*After that Culprit throws the thing . . .*]

As you've all seen, a horrible crime has been committed, and we've rounded up these five suspects. Victim, I want you to ask each person in the lineup whether they threw the thing. And, folks, normally I wouldn't promote lying, but for the purposes of this game, you may lie about whether or not you threw it. Let's see if our Victim can determine who actually did the deed.

[*After the Interrogation, ask the Victim to name the Culprit.*]

Why did you choose that person? (A guilty look? Past history? Crowd reaction?)

[*Name the Culprit.*]

I imagine that this sort of thing might go on in your home every so often, with Mom or Dad doing the Interrogation. Of course none of you would ever lie about doing anything wrong?! But even if you did, parents have a way of figuring out guilt.

Have you found this true? Have your parents ever guessed your guilt? (Maybe not. But they might have some stories of being found out.)

Bible Discovery

If you want to know how guilt started, turn to the first book of the Bible, Genesis. In chapter 2 we find God creating man, putting him in the Garden of Eden with one simple command; Don't eat of the Tree of the Knowledge of Good and Evil.

In chapter 3 we find the tempter coming in the form of a serpent. I imagine you know the story. The serpent tempted Eve first, then she shared with Adam. Let's read the story beginning in Genesis 3:6. Someone read verses 6-8.

According to these verses, what happened immediately after they ate the forbidden fruit? (Their eyes were opened; they realized they were naked; they covered themselves.)

How would you describe that feeling, right after they sinned? (Guilt? Shame? Embarrassment?)

Some of you are kind of tickled that we said the word *naked*. Unfortunately, this gives some people the wrong idea that the original sin was all about sex. It wasn't. It was about disobedience, rebellion. And for the first time ever, people felt shame.

So then in verse 8 we see God coming out for his daily stroll with them in the Garden. Why do you think Adam and Eve hid? (Did they think if they avoided the issue, it would go away?)

Notice that no one has judged them yet. They haven't been scolded for their sin. They simply did something they knew was wrong, and now they feel bad about it.

So, in just these few verses, what are the two things they have tried to do as a result of their sin? (They tried to cover up. They tried to hide.)

Do people do those same things nowadays when they do something wrong? How? (It's hard to look someone in the eye if you've wronged someone. Or you avoid them.)

In what ways do we also hide from God?

Some people come to God pretending to be something they're not. They cover themselves with religious words and nice clothes, but they're never really honest with God. They're guilty of sin, but they're trying to cover over it.

Other people run away from God. They know they've done some pretty messed-up things, and they know God doesn't like it. So they don't go to church, they stop hanging with Christians, they never pray or read the Bible. They're hiding from God.

Jesus told a story about two men who went to the Temple to pray. One was a Pharisee, a big-time religious leader. He stood proudly and prayed, "Lord, I thank you that I'm not like those sinners out there. Look at all the religious things I do."

The second man was a tax-collector. Nowadays he'd be a loan shark or a mob boss – a pretty obvious sinner. He wouldn't even raise his eyes to heaven, but he knelt and prayed, "Lord, have mercy on me. I know I'm a sinner."

Jesus said that God honored the prayer of the tax collector and not the Pharisee. The Pharisee was covering up his sin. And no doubt there were other tax collectors who were hiding from God. They didn't bother to come to the Temple. But this man came and laid his guilt before the Lord. There's one more detail we should look at before we leave Genesis 3.

What did Adam and Eve cover themselves with? (Fig leaves.)

Now look at Genesis 3:21. What does God give them to wear? (Animal skins.)

You have to kill an animal to use the skin. I know some of you are animal-lovers, and this seems gruesome, but even here at the beginning, God was making an important point: *sin brings death*. When you sin, something dies. Maybe a relationship dies. Maybe your innocence dies. But you can't cover it up by sewing together a fig-leaf swimsuit. It takes a death to pay for the death that sin causes. That's how serious sin is.

Turn to Leviticus 6. Would someone read verses 1-5?

If you lived in ancient Israel and you were guilty of any sin that people do, what were you supposed to do? (Pay it back, plus twenty percent.)

So let's say I come to you asking, "Have you seen ten dollars lying around here?" You deny any knowledge of the money. But the truth is, you picked up that ten-dollar bill in this very room last week. After a few days, you feel very guilty about the whole deal, and you want to set it right.

According to these verses, how can you set it right? (Pay me twelve bucks. Restitution plus one-fifth.)

But wait, there's more. Would somebody read verses 6-7?

What else would you have to do? (Bring a ram from your flock to the priest.)

The priest will sacrifice the ram on the altar because you've not only sinned against the other person. You've sinned against God. Sin brings death. And so death is the only way to pay for sin.

Turn to Leviticus 16. Actually there are several passages in Leviticus that talk about different types of sacrifices, but this is an interesting one. The priest would select two goats for this offering. Somebody read verses 7-10.

What happened to the goats? (One was killed. The other was set free.)

Maybe you've heard the word "scapegoat." This is where it comes from. Two goats were presented to the Lord, and one was randomly chosen to die, while the other was set free. There are two different things God does with our sin. He forgives it, through the sacrifice of blood, but he also drives it away. The scapegoat symbolically took the people's sin upon itself and ran off into the desert with it, never to be seen again.

But I want you to get another picture in mind, too. There were two goats. One was killed and the other was set free. In the same way, Christ was our sacrifice. He died so that we could be set free.

Turn to Isaiah 1. As I said, there were different types of sacrifices, some for different occasions, different times of year, different types of sin. First at the Tabernacle and later when they built the big Temple, people would come with animals to be offered in payment for their sins. But there was a problem. Would someone read what God says in Isaiah 1:11-13?

This is the Lord talking here. What did he think about their sacrifices? (He had no pleasure in them. They were meaningless.)

Would someone read verses 16-17?

What do you think they were doing wrong? (Apparently they were not seeking justice in society. They were ignoring the needs of the poor – the orphans and widows.)

So . . . what was wrong with their sacrifices? Why were they meaningless? (Because the sacrifices weren't connected with any commitment of the heart. The people performed the rituals to atone for their sin, but then they continued the same sinful practices. They weren't really sorry for their sin.)

There are a number of religious actions that people do today – taking communion, singing worship songs, donating money, etc. Sometimes people get the wrong idea that these actions pay for their sins in some way. They think they can score points with God, so he lets them slide on some misdemeanors. But it doesn't work like that, God says in Isaiah. Would somebody read Isaiah 1:18?

What is God saying here? (He wants people to meet with him and discuss how he'll take away their sin.)

Do you ever treat God like a machine when he really wants a personal conversation?

For instance . . . going to church each week is important. We know God likes that. But why? He wants to meet you there. But if you're passing notes or daydreaming, do you score points with God merely by being there?

Not really. Stop treating him like some time clock that you punch in to. He wants a personal conversation.

Some people feel very guilty about things they've done. Maybe you're like that. And sometimes they do some religious things to make them feel better – they go to church, pray, do some good deeds. And maybe these distract them for a while, but they don't really pay for the sin. The guilt feelings are still there.

But here we have the assurance that the sin can be taken away, but there's only one way. Not by good deeds. Not by some religious machine. But by the blood of Jesus Christ. His death paid the ultimate price for our sin. And now we can live free. Would someone read Hebrews 10:19-22?

What attitude is described here? How do we approach God? (With confidence, assurance, because we're cleansed from a guilty conscience.)

According to verse 22, what should we do in response to Jesus' sacrifice? (Draw near to God.)

God wants a relationship with us. Not one where we cower in guilt and fear, but a relationship where we can stand confidently in the assurance that he has cleansed us of our sins.

So What?

Leader's Note

Break into groups of 4-6 and distribute the "Guilty as Sin" Handout. They should read the case and discuss what they'd say to the person. Have each group start with a different case study (A-B-C-D) and cycle back to A if there's time. After 8-10 minutes, bring the groups back together to discuss their ideas. There are some suggestions below to help discussion.

A **My best friend and I tried out for the school musical. She's really good, but somehow I got the lead role and she was just put in the chorus. Now it's hard to talk with her, because I feel guilty for getting the part she wanted.**

What would you say? There may be guilt *feelings*, but there's no actual guilt here. You did nothing wrong. You did your best at an audition, and you got a good role. You don't have to feel bad about winning a competition fair and square.

Still, what do you do with these feelings of guilt? How can you make them go away? First, *talk to yourself.* Are you actually guilty? If not, tell yourself that. Second, *rename the feeling.* You feel "bad," but that doesn't have to be guilt. It could be sympathy for your friend who didn't get the part. That's a healthy feeling to have. Third, *keep that relationship healthy.* If possible, talk about your feelings with your friend. Encourage her. If she is trying to use your guilt feelings against you, you might avoid her for a little while.

B **There was this new kid in school who was kind of weird, so a bunch of us picked on him. I'm not proud of this. This kid wound up being my lab partner, so I guess I said a lot of mean things to him. I didn't want anyone else to think we were friends. Anyway, the kid dropped out of school, and I heard he's in a hospital or something. I feel bad about the whole thing, but I don't know what I can do about it.**

What would you say? Your guilt is healthy. It's an alarm going off. You were wrong to pick on this kid, and now you feel bad because it apparently caused more damage than you intended. Let's think about four steps toward healing.

(1) *Repentance.* Are you sorry for what you did? Not just because of the results, but because it was wrong? If so, tell God you're sorry and ask for his forgiveness.

(2) *Restitution.* Can you do anything to make amends? It might not be possible, but give it a try. Can you find the kid's family and send a note of apology? That would be a gutsy thing to do, and it might help their healing process.

(3) *Sacrifice.* You don't have to do anything to win God's forgiveness, but it might help you to understand the seriousness of your sin if you do something special to focus on God. Make a donation. Go to a prayer meeting at church. Schedule 15 minutes alone with God, on your knees. You can be creative here. It's just a physical way to say, "I was wrong, and I'm sorry."

(4) *New Commitment.* Promise God that you'll try not to do this again. In fact, you might use this experience as a reason to make an extra effort to befriend new kids at school. True repentance leads to life change.

C **My dad left a couple months ago, and now my mom's a mess. They've been fighting for a long time, so I guess it's no surprise that they're finally getting divorced. The problem is, I've had a tough year myself. I've been getting in trouble at school and really nasty to both Mom and Dad. Now I'm feeling guilty, like maybe I pushed them over the edge. If I were a better kid, maybe they'd still be together.**

What would you say? This is a very common feeling among kids whose parents are divorcing. You're not strange to feel this way, but you're wrong. You are not the reason your parents split up. They had their own issues. If you don't believe this, ask them point blank. It's not your fault.

It still stinks. And you will be feeling all sorts of strange things over the next year or two – anger, sadness, sudden hopes that are suddenly dashed. It will be tough enough for you to deal with, without heaping guilt on top. This is a case where the guilt feelings don't match up with the reality.

And by the way, those behavior problems you've had over the past year, they were probably your emotional response to your parents' difficulties. That doesn't give you an excuse to misbehave, but it might explain it a little. You've had some crazy events sparking crazy emotions, and you chose to express yourself in bad ways.

A suggestion: Find a counselor to help you through this. Your mom or dad might connect you with a professional counselor. Your pastor or youth pastor might also provide help, or you might get some guidance from a school counselor. You need someone you can trust to help you make better choices during this tough time.

D **I had been keeping myself pure for marriage. Notice the past tense. Last month my parents were away, so my boyfriend came over, and it seemed so perfect. The next morning I began to realize what we had done, but I tried to pretend like everything was fine. In the last week or two, I've been feeling guiltier and guiltier. I broke up with the guy, because every time I saw him, I**

remembered our sin. Now I feel like I'm the dirtiest person on earth. How can I go to church like this, or even pray? I'd be such a hypocrite.

What would you say? You feel guilty because you are guilty. You sinned, and you know it. Now, what can you do about it? So far, you're avoiding the best options. You *can* go to church, and you *have* to pray. Church is where sinful people go to meet a forgiving God.

And God longs for you to come to him in prayer. He knows you messed up. Now he wants to work with you to put things back together. Read Isaiah 1:18 again. He wants to "reason together" with you and cleanse you of your sin.

You lost something very important to you, your purity, and you will feel sorrow over what you've lost. But you can still enjoy a deep relationship with God. You can still serve him in powerful ways. He delights in forgiving sins and restoring broken souls.

Earlier we mentioned a plan of Repentance-Restitution-Sacrifice-Commitment. That plan will be helpful to you. First, tell God you're sorry. Then it might help you to talk with your former boyfriend and set things straight – you both did wrong, and that can't happen again. (He doesn't need to agree, but you may need to say that.) Spend special time with God. Finally, promise God that you'll try to live in a new purity.

Just Do It

I want you to think about something that you feel guilty for. Maybe you don't feel guilty at all, and that's fine. You don't need to invent something. But if you do have guilt feelings, turn your handout over and write down what that is. You might want to use a code word because this is really between you and God.

The first thing you need to do is to see how your guilt feelings match up with reality. Are you feeling guilty because you are guilty, or is there some other emotional thing going on? Or maybe you're not sure.

If your guilt feelings come from something you did wrong, ***are you sorry for what you did?*** If so, then write down the words, "Lord, I'm sorry." That's where repentance begins.

Do you need to make restitution? Did you hurt somebody else? Can you make things right? If so, write down something you can do to make restitution.

Is there some action you can take as a "sacrifice?" This would be some good thing you would do to remind yourself that you sinned and to show God you're sorry. Let me repeat: This is not a way to earn God's forgiveness. That has already been paid for, through the blood of Christ. This is simply a physical way to demonstrate your sorrow for sin and focus back on God. Think of something creative, something appropriate, and write that down too.

Can you make a commitment to avoid making the same mistake? Oh, you might fail again. But you want to tell God of your desire to please him. If this is your desire, write down.

As we close, take one more look at what you've written, and talk with God about it.

03 pleading guilty

Objectives

- Group members will learn from the book of Romans about guilt, sin, atonement, and sanctification.
- They will consider how they can live a guilt-free life.

Bible Reference

Romans 2:14-15; 3:9,21-24; 5:1,6,8; 6:1-2,21-23; 7:19-25; 8:1,9-11,15-16.

Preparation

Go to www.BlueFishTV.com/Handouts and click Revolution Volume 1. Then click on the *Pleading Guilty* lesson to download "*Re:Verse*" handout and make copies for the whole class; pens/pencils.

Startup

Think of some trouble you got into when you were 10 years old or younger – something you did wrong. Can you think of something? I want you to picture exactly what you did, and maybe how you got caught. Now who would like to share that with the group? Come on up here and tell us about it. No, wait. Why don't you act it out instead? Without words.

Leader's Note *You may have to start with your own scene of childhood pranks. Hopefully, you'll have a few students offering their scenes. After each one, ask them to explain what they were acting out, or see if the group can guess. We don't want to make light of misbehavior, but you'll probably be seeing scenes of silly pranks. If there is something more serious, use the opportunity to talk about it.*

As in the previous sessions, we're talking about guilt. You may have felt guilty after getting in the trouble you were just remembering. Maybe you still feel guilty. In any case, I imagine that you've done other things since then that make you feel even guiltier. So, where does that guilt come from? And where does it go? Let's look into Scripture to find out.

Bible Discovery

Turn to Romans 2. We're going to spend a lot of time in this book today. In Romans, Paul presents the case for Christ. Why do we need a Savior? Why should we trust Jesus? Like a good lawyer, Paul builds his arguments.

First we need to know that Paul was writing to a mixed group of Jews and Gentiles. The Jews had the law and prided themselves on how well they kept it. Gentiles – of course that's the term for all non-Jews – knew nothing about the law. But Paul suggests that they have another law. Would someone read Romans 2:14-15?

We're picking up the argument in the middle, and Paul is talking like a lawyer, so don't be bothered if you don't quite follow it. Zero in on verse 15.

Where are the requirements of the law written? (On their hearts. That is, on *our* hearts.)

This is like a courtroom drama. You're the defendant. What role does your conscience play? (It's a witness. And it either testifies for you or against you.)

Let's put this all together. Paul is talking to Jews, who know what's good and bad from the Scriptures, and to Gentiles, who at that time didn't know the Scriptures. But Paul says that all of us, even Gentiles, still know what's good and bad, because it's written on our hearts. Our conscience tells us whether we're doing right or wrong.

Who gave you your conscience? (God did. That's how we're made.)

So you have a built-in mechanism that can make you feel guilty when you're guilty. We've talked about this as a kind of "moral alarm system." It goes off when something is wrong. Now this alarm mechanism can get fried, or it can become over-sensitive, but the basic apparatus is something everybody has, no matter what religion they follow.

Now back to Romans. Paul is making the point that everyone on earth has the ability to know what's right and wrong. That sets up his next point. Would someone read Romans 3:9?

Who is "under sin"? (Jews and Gentiles alike.)

Would someone read Romans 3:23?

If all have sinned, who has a reason to feel guilty? (Everyone.)

So how can we get rid of this guilt? That's where the book of Romans is taking us. In fact, if we pull back the lens and look at the last verse in context, we'll see. Someone read Romans 3:21-24.

How can we get rid of our guilt? (Through faith in Jesus.)

Take a look at the beginning of verse 25. What's a sacrifice of atonement? (Just as the priests offered up the blood of an animal to pay for the people's sin, so God offered up the blood of Jesus, to pay for everyone's sin. In fact, the Bible tells us that those animal sacrifices were just symbols of the coming sacrifice of Jesus.)

Would somebody read Romans 5:1?

What does it mean to be "justified"? (Made right. You might think of it as "*Just as if I'd* never sinned.")

According to this verse, what's the result of being justified? (We have peace with God.)

When you feel guilty, isn't that what you want? You want God to come down, put his hand on your shoulder, and say, "It's all right. I'll take care of it. No problem." You want the peace of knowing that your wrong has been made right.

Somebody read Romans 5:6.

Who did Christ die for? (The ungodly.)

Let's check Romans 5:8. Somebody read that for us.

How does God show his love? (Christ died for us, as sinners.)

Why would he do that? Why would he offer this justification to sinners? (Because we're the ones who need it. Because, as we saw before, all of us are sinners. If he didn't save sinners, there would be no one to save.)

Sometimes we get the idea that, if you're good enough, God will take your guilt away. People think that you have to become a good person for God to save you. But that makes no sense. Essentially it would mean that we would be saving ourselves. But as we just read in Romans 5:6, we are "powerless." We can't be good enough for God. Besides, if we're asking God to make something right, we have to admit that it's wrong.

So if you're feeling guilty because you've done something wrong – good! God has you right where he wants you. Oh, it's not good that you did something bad, but that's in the past now. In this moment, your guilt alarm is going off, you know you're a sinner, and you know you need God's help. You want "peace with God" and you know that the only way to get that is to claim Jesus' blood as the payment for your sin. God can make things right.

Let's take a moment right now to go through that personally. A few of you may be tracking with me. You are feeling guilty, and you need God's grace to forgive you. Why not claim his forgiveness right now?

Follow the Spirit's leading in this moment. You might pause for silent prayer, or you might voice a prayer for forgiveness, which they could pray silently with you. Or the Spirit might have some other idea.

Well, that was easy. You sin, you pray, you're forgiven. Peace with God. Great! Now you can go out and commit the same sin all over again, right? Let's see what Paul has to say about that. Would someone read Romans 6:1-2?

What is he asking in verse 1? (If God forgives us for our sin, why shouldn't we keep sinning? In fact, Paul is setting it up even more strongly: If we praise God for the grace that forgives our sin, shouldn't we sin more so we can praise him more?)

What's the answer? ("No way!" is an appropriate translation. "May it never be!")

Why is that such a ridiculous question? What is Paul's logic here? (We are dead to sin. Why should we go back to it? Why would you keep living in sin when you don't have to?)

Take a look at verses 3-4. Paul paints a picture for us. Sin brings death, right? So Jesus dies on the cross because of our sin, and then he's buried in the tomb. But it's like we are buried with him. But then what happened to Jesus? He rose from the dead to give us new life. So it's like we're raised from the dead with him.

Now when we sin, it's like we're going back into the tomb. Oh, he'll forgive us again, we know that, but when you've got this great resurrected life, why would you want to go back into the tomb? Would someone read Romans 6:21-23?

What's the difference between the sinful life and the godly life? (The sinful life is deadly. The godly life brings life. The sinful life is shameful. The godly life is holy.)

Is the sinful life really deadly? How? As you look at the sinful behavior around you, does it really bring death? (In its various forms, sin destroys, deforms, and kills. Obviously murder is a sin that literally kills life. But lying kills the truth. Pride destroys the spirit. Hateful words can kill the hopes of someone else. Selfishness can destroy relationships. Sin brings death, not just as punishment, but in its very essence.)

So we have a choice: the way of life or the way of death. So naturally we'll choose the way of life all the time, right? Right? Won't we always choose to do the right thing? No? How can we possibly choose the deadly way of sin when Jesus raises us to new life? Well, we're not the only ones with that problem. Would someone read Romans 7:19-21?

Have you ever experienced this? You want to do good, but you do evil instead?

Leader's Note

You might want to be ready with your own example.

How did Paul explain this kind of "double life?" What was really responsible for the bad things he did? ("Sin living in me.")

Of course it's not just Paul. All of us deal with this evil force inside us. In verse 18, Paul calls it the "sinful nature." The literal word he uses is "flesh"—that part of us that cares only about feeding the appetite, getting what we want, me first. It's a struggle, isn't it, responding to God's direction while at the same time dealing with the urges of the sinful nature. Sometimes the right thing is staring us in the face, we're just about to make the good choice, and *wham!* We get blindsided by desire and we do exactly the wrong thing.

After describing this struggle for a while, Paul erupts with a gut-wrenching question. Would somebody read Romans 7:24?

What does Paul want? (Rescue from this "body of death." Who can kill the alien inside us?)

Take a look at verse 25. Is there an answer to the question? Who will rescue us? ("Jesus Christ our Lord" is the answer. And yet even this answer doesn't make the struggle go away. We may want to serve God, but we still find our sinful appetites luring us away.)

When you consider that even the apostle Paul was struggling with sinful behavior, what do you think about your own struggles? (It might make you feel a little better. It's still a struggle, but you're in good company.)

The next chapter might make you feel even better. Somebody read Romans 8:1-2.

How much will God condemn you for your struggle with sin? (Not at all.) **No, really?** (Really.) **We were just talking about sinful appetites, about how we know what's right and do what's wrong. God has to condemn us for that, doesn't he?** (No.)

There is no condemnation . . . for whom? (Those who are in Christ Jesus.)

How can there be no condemnation? (Because of Jesus. He forgives our sin, through his blood. His sacrifice pays for all our sin.)

Are you a Christian? Have you asked Christ into your life? Then you are "in Christ Jesus," and he is in you. And you will have a struggle, because the Spirit of Christ will be calling you to do the things that bring life and love and joy, while your sinful nature keeps promoting destructive choices. Sometimes you may fail, but God will not condemn you. He will challenge you, he will teach you, he may let you experience the bad results of your bad choices, but he will also forgive you.

But there's hope for this struggle we're in, because the power of Christ within us is ultimately stronger than the power of our sinful desires. Would someone read verses 9-11?

So who has the upper hand in this struggle? (The Spirit of God.)

What does Jesus' resurrection have to do with anything? (It's the Spirit of the one who raised Jesus' body out of the tomb. He certainly has the power to raise us out of our slavery to the deeds of death. The resurrection is a picture of what happens to us every time we make the right choice instead of the wrong one. The Spirit pulls us out of death and into life.)

So What?

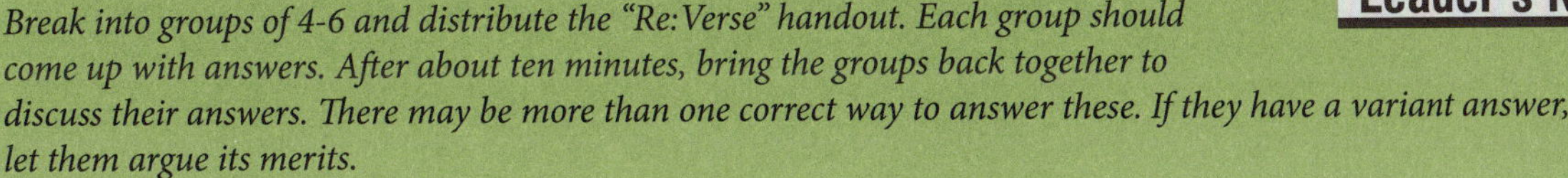

Leader's Note

Break into groups of 4-6 and distribute the "Re:Verse" handout. Each group should come up with answers. After about ten minutes, bring the groups back together to discuss their answers. There may be more than one correct way to answer these. If they have a variant answer, let them argue its merits.

What was your answer? And why did you choose that?

1. *It's not a bad gig, as I see it. I party all Friday and Saturday night, get totally wasted, but then I go to church Sunday and get forgiven. Then more parties the next weekend.*

Preferred Answer: D
This person needs to know that God not only forgives us, but he calls us to a new kind of life.

2. *It's always such a struggle to do the right thing. Just when I think I've succeeded, I fall down again. The temptation is so strong, how can I ever get it right?*

Preferred Answer: H
This person needs strength to fight temptation. It will help to know that Jesus' resurrection power is available.

3. *The kids at my school are so bad, I can't stand them. I hate to be around them. I'm so glad I'm not immoral like they are.*

Preferred Answer: A
This person is falling into the pride trap. "Good" people commit sin too. (B would also be an accepted response.)

4. *I try to be a good Christian, but you don't understand: I have to have sex. It's like God made me this way. Why should I stop?*

Preferred Answer: E
This person needs a challenge to dedicate his or her body to God's purposes.

5. *I'm a Christian; I should know better. But after what I did, I must be going straight to hell. I don't know if I can ever pray again.*

Preferred Answer: G

"No condemnation!" That's the message this person desperately needs to hear.

6. *I like it when you say that Jesus loves me, but you don't know how bad I am. There's no way I can be the kind of person Jesus loves.*

Preferred Answer: C

This person is exactly the kind of person Jesus loves – a sinner.

7. *It's a battle out there. We're fighting for righteousness and they're fighting for evil. We just have to win.*

Preferred Answer: B

Sure, there are struggles, but when we fight too hard, we lose our sense of humble service. This person needs a reminder that all have sinned. (A would also be an accepted response.)

8. *I feel so guilty. I've sinned again, even though I knew it was wrong. I have no excuses. How can God forgive me?*

Preferred Answer: F

This person needs to know that this struggle is a common one, faced even by the apostle Paul. Keep working at it. Receive God's forgiveness, and tap into more and more of his strength.

Just Do It

What have we learned here? How would you sum up the message of Romans?

Here are some points:

- God wants us to live right
- He knows we don't always live right
- He forgives us for sin
- He wants us to live free and forgiven
- He knows we still struggle
- He doesn't condemn us, because of Jesus
- He gives us the Spirit to help us live right

Take a look at those sayings on the worksheet, not the verses, but the other side. Do you know people who are saying those things? Maybe you *are* saying those things. But is there someone else in your world who needs the assurance, the peace, or the challenge of one of those verses? Think about how you could share that.

And I know some of you still struggle with guilt. You know God wants you to do what's right, and you feel very bad whenever you do wrong. In closing, let me offer some words of assurance.
[*Read Romans 8:15-16 aloud.*]

04 worry

Objectives

- Group members will learn from the video about feelings of anxiety and depression, seeing good and bad ways to handle these feelings.
- In the lesson, they will be prompted to consider their own feelings of anxiety and depression, finding God-based ways to cope.

Bible Reference

Matthew 6:25-34; assorted verses of assurance and hope.

Preparation

Go to www.BlueFishTV.com/Handouts and click Revolution Volume 1. Then click on the *Worry* lesson to download "*From Bad to Verse*" handout and make copies for the whole class; set up TV/DVD player; *Worry* DVD; pens/pencils.

Startup

What are you concerned about in school these days? I know you may have stuff going on in your home or in your relationships, but let's just talk about school. What's the biggest worry you have there?

Leader's Note

Go around the circle and see what they're concerned about. A test coming up, a project, an inconsistent teacher, making the team, getting into college. Don't judge or preach, but listen to their concerns. You could also make some notes to pray about these matters and check back later to see how things went.

Concern, worry, anxiety – there are different levels. Some of the things you talked about were mild concerns. You want it to go well, but it's not a huge thing. Other matters are pretty huge, and you're thinking about them a lot. And what happens when you get five or six "concerns" at the same time? These things can add up.

Showtime

Show *Worry* video

Re:view

How would you define "anxiety"? (Doug Fields defined anxiety this way: "Anxiety is fearing something about our future that we can't control.")

Doug Fields mentioned that there are 365 verses in the Bible that say, "Fear not," in one way or another. Why do you think there are so many? (Some of these statements occur in stories where God or angels appear to people and they scare them silly. But in many other cases, God is telling people – and telling us – to trust him rather than focusing on the frightful circumstances.)

In the video, we heard that great verse, Philippians 4:6 – "Don't worry about anything. Instead, pray about everything." How can that attitude change your life? (Instead of obsessing about the circumstances, we bring the matter before the Lord. That brings us face to face with his strength. That can help to calm us down.)

Does prayer really "work?" Can we count on prayer to change the situations we're worried about? Will prayer make things happen the way we want? (Sometimes prayers are answered just the way we want, but usually there's a lot more going on. Prayer can change situations, but it primarily changes *us*, by bringing us into the presence of our awesome God. Often, our anxiety makes situations worse. But when we pray, we're responding in faith, and that may help us deal better with our situations.)

At one point Doug said that prayer is "upside-down worry." What did he mean by that? (It's a cool picture. When we worry, the circumstances of life press down on us, because we can't control them. But flip that over and suddenly God lifts us above our circumstances. When we pray, we are putting God on top and leaving our problems beneath us.)

In the video, we saw some different ways people were dealing with anxiety. What do the people around you do to cope with their worries? (People get drunk or they do drugs as a way of escape. Kids are cutting themselves or developing eating disorders, possibly as a way to control *something* about their lives. Others get lost in wild behavior, risk-taking, or sexual experimentation to distract them from their problems. Others put on a cynicism or an over-confidence or a rebellious spirit to cover over their fears.)

Does it help matters to get drunk or high? Why or why not? (It may distract people for a night, but it doesn't make the problems go away. It just makes them worse. As Weston said in the video, "Right when you're back sober again, all the problems are back. . . and the stress was there and it was even heavier than before.")

Rather than engaging in destructive behavior, like getting drunk or cutting, Doug said we should seek out the root cause of the problem. How do you do that? (Sometimes that takes counseling – either professionally or with a wise teacher or youth leader. Sometimes you can deal with it by talking it out with friends. It helps to understand that most of that destructive behavior is an escape from something else or a covering for something else. Are you angry? Are you worried? Are you sad? Then what are you angry, worried, or sad about? If you can answer those questions honestly, you can express those emotions in healthy ways.)

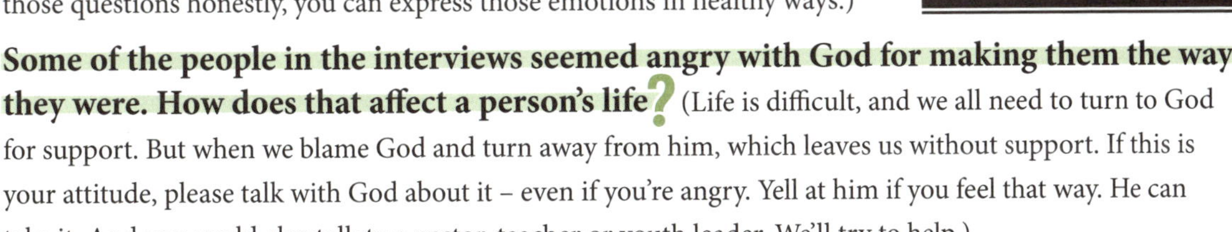

Some of the people in the interviews seemed angry with God for making them the way they were. How does that affect a person's life? (Life is difficult, and we all need to turn to God for support. But when we blame God and turn away from him, which leaves us without support. If this is your attitude, please talk with God about it – even if you're angry. Yell at him if you feel that way. He can take it. And you could also talk to a pastor, teacher or youth leader. We'll try to help.)

One of the things that came through was the importance of hope. What is hope? How would you define it? How does it compare with anxiety? (If anxiety is "fearing something about our future that we can't control," then hope is knowing that God is in control of the future. We know that he loves us and he wants what's best for us.)

How do you get hope? (Keep in close relationship with God. When you find yourself obsessing about all the things that can go wrong, bring those worries to God and get his perspective. Surround yourself with other believers who trust God to care for them. They will encourage you – and you can encourage them.)

Just Do It

Turn to Matthew 6:25. Would someone read verses 25-26?

What did Jesus say we shouldn't worry about? (What you eat or drink or wear.)

If he were speaking at an assembly in your school, what do you think he would say you shouldn't worry about? (Your grades. Your college or work plans. Who you're going to date. Whether your clothes are cool enough.)

Somebody read verses 31-32.

When it comes to worrying, what's the difference between "pagans" and believers? (Pagans, those who don't know God, worry about the stuff of life, how they can get more and more. Believers know that God cares for them and will provide what they need.)

Somebody read verses 33-34.

As Christians what should we be most concerned with? (God's kingdom.)

When we make God's kingdom our top priority, what will happen? (All our needs will be provided for.)

What does that mean? What is God's "kingdom?" How do we seek it? (God's kingdom is wherever God is in charge. It's whatever He wants. When we seek the kingdom, we're putting his desires first.)

Leader's Note *Distribute the "From Bad to Verse" handout, along with index cards.*

There was a good idea that emerged in the video. At times when you're worried, it might help to have one of God's promises close by, something you can read to get the reassurance you need.

So I'll ask you to gather in groups of twos and threes. Take turns looking up these verses. When you hear one that could really be helpful to you, jot it down on a card. Then take these home with you and keep them in places where you need them – your notebook, your locker, your computer, your bedroom – wherever.

[*If there is time, you could ask for volunteers to share their special verse.*]

05 hi, anxiety

Objectives

- Group members will learn from various Old Testament Scriptures about people who were dealing with a lot of pressures, emotionally and physically.
- From those examples, group members will consider how they can deal with the pressures in their lives.

Bible Reference

Genesis 4:13-15; Genesis 32; Exodus 18:13-26; Ruth 1:1-18; 4:13-15; 1 Samuel 24; 1 Kings 19:1-18; Psalm 46; Esther 3:8-9; 4:11-16; 8:7; Daniel 6:3-23.

Preparation

Go to www.BlueFishTV.com/Handouts and click Revolution Volume 1. Then click on the *Hi, Anxiety* lesson to download "*Coping*" handout and make copies for the whole class; 20 or more random items for the opening activity (see below); chalkboard or equivalent; pens/pencils.

Startup

Have you ever gone to the store to get just a few things, so you don't get a cart or a basket, but then you see something else you like, and then something else? Before you know it, you're balancing armfuls of stuff as you stagger to the "10 Items or Less" lane. We're going to have a little competition based on that experience. I need a couple of volunteers.

Leader's Note

The success of this game starts with the selection of objects. Get about 20 items of different shapes and sizes without handles – a box, a book, a cup of water, a hula hoop, a newspaper, a whiffleball bat, etc. Try to keep everything light. Put the volunteer in front, and hand them items one by one, with the group keeping count. You might try this with 2 or 3 volunteers, seeing who can hold the most items.

Life is like the game we just played. In what way? (Each of us has to deal with a lot of stuff in our lives – daily stress of school, work, and home; emotional issues of relationships; spiritual ups and downs; etc. How can we handle everything – especially when those things don't come with handles?)

Bible Discovery

We're going to look at biblical examples of people who were dealing with a lot of stuff. Turn to Genesis 4:13.

What do you know about Cain and Abel? (The main thing is that Cain got jealous and murdered his brother Abel.)

Of course God found out about it – he always does – and he confronted Cain. You might remember the scene. God says, "Cain, where's your brother?"

Do you remember how Cain answered? ("I don't know. Am I my brother's keeper?")

God went on to announce his judgment upon Cain, the murderer. But let's read what Cain said in verses 13-14. Someone read that aloud.

What was Cain's complaint? (His punishment was too great.)

We've all felt that way. We admit that we're guilty, but we think the punishment is too severe. But wait a second! Cain is a murderer! Where does he get the nerve to ask for leniency? What do you think God did in response to this crazy complaint? Well, somebody read his response in verse 15.

How does God respond? (He agrees to put a mark of protection on Cain. Cain will still have to wander the earth, but no one will kill him.)

What does that tell you about God? (He is just, but also merciful. He judges sin, but he also cares for the people he judges.)

Today we're talking about people who had a lot to deal with. In these verses, what was Cain dealing with? (A life sentence that would almost certainly become a death sentence.)

What did he do about it? (He complained to God. While he didn't specifically ask for anything, the whole tone of his complaint seems to be a cry for help, asking for God's mercy.)

Do you ever feel like complaining to God? Do you think that's a good thing to do? (It seems disrespectful, but the truth is that many people in the Bible did so. Many good people. God is not our butler, responding to our orders, but he does care how we feel.)

If you have a chalkboard available, write "Ask God for help."

Leader's Note

So here's one option for us, as we deal with all the stuff in our lives. Cry for help – even if you got yourself in the mess to begin with. If God could help Cain, who killed his own brother, he can help you. Turn to Genesis 32. Would someone read verses 3-6?

Jacob was on the move, with all his family, flocks, and possessions. He had been staying with his father-in-law for twenty years, and now it was time to forge out on his own. But there was one problem: his brother Esau.

What do you know about the relationship between Jacob and Esau? (Jacob had tricked Esau out of the rights of the firstborn child, and he received the blessing of his blind father by pretending to be Esau. When Esau heard about that, he vowed revenge, and Jacob had to flee. That was the last time they had seen each other.)

Jacob knew he needed to confront the Esau problem, so he sent his brother a message. What was the report he got back? (Esau was on his way, with 400 men.)

How do you think Jacob felt about that? Look at verses 7-8 for some clues. (Jacob had "fear and distress." Assuming that Esau would attack him, he divided his stuff into two groups. If Esau attacked one, Jacob could flee with the other.)

Take a look at verse 11. Just as Cain did earlier, Jacob cried out to God for help. The next day he had a new plan. He sent his flocks ahead as gifts to Esau. In fact, he sent his whole family ahead, and by nightfall, he was all alone. Somebody read Genesis 32:24-26.

Who won this wrestling match? (Looks like Jacob, though he dislocated his hip.)

This is a strange story, and there are various interpretations. Jacob encountered some supernatural being – an angel, or perhaps some manifestation of God himself – and wrestled with him. It was a tough match, but Jacob grabbed his opponent and would not let go until he got a blessing. Somebody read verses 27-29.

Did Jacob get his blessing? (Yes, but he got more. His name was changed. *Jacob* means "Grabber," and he spent his whole life grabbing stuff – from Esau, from his father-in-law, from everyone. But *Israel* means "One Who Struggles with God." He was still grabbing, in a way, but he was grabbing for God.)

What do you think happened with Esau? (Look at 33:4 for the answer. They had a peaceful meeting, like long-lost brothers.)

Write on the chalkboard, "Wrestle with God."

Leader's Note

What could this mean in your life? How can you wrestle with God? (Grab for God in every experience of life. Where is he pushing you? How do you respond? If you've got a question, complaint, or confusion, don't hide it. Take it to him.)

Leader's Note *Distribute the "Coping" handout. Break into groups of 4-6, assigning 2-3 characters to each group. It's fine if certain characters are studied by more than one group, but make sure all the characters are covered. Give them 10-12 minutes to work on this, then bring them back together for discussion.*

Assignments

A. Moses (Exodus 18:13-26)

B. Ruth (Ruth 1:1-18; result: Ruth 4:13-15)

C. David (1 Samuel 24:1-12; result: verses 16-22)

D. Elijah (1 Kings 19:1-18; background: chapter 18)

E. Esther (Esther 4:11-16; background: Esther 3:8-9; result: Esther 8:7)

F. Daniel (Daniel 6:3-23)

Moses (*Exodus 18:13-26*)

What was this person dealing with?

He had too much work to do, as judge and leader of this nation.

How did he or she deal with it?

At his father-in-law's suggestion, he appointed a team of leaders to rule over groups of the people.

What was the result?

Jethro predicted that "you will be able to stand the strain, and all these people will go home satisfied." The result would be Moses' own health and efficiency in government.

Leader's Note *Write on the board: "Get others to help."*

Ruth (*Ruth 1:1-18; result: Ruth 4:13-15*)

What was this person dealing with?

Famine. The death of her husband. Now her mother-in-law wanted to move.

How did he or she deal with it?

She clung to an important relationship. She had obviously grown to love her mother-in-law, and apparently she had come to share her faith in God.

What was the result?
The story ends with Naomi happy at last. Ruth is happily married and bearing a son, who will become an ancestor of King David, and ultimately Jesus.

Leader's Note 

Write on the board: "Cling to God-honoring relationships."

David (*1 Samuel 24:1-12; result: verses 16-22*)

What was this person dealing with?
David was running for his life from a crazy king.

How did he or she deal with it?
He had a chance to kill King Saul, but he refused. That went against his principles. Saul was still God's appointed king, and it wasn't up to David to seize the throne.

What was the result?
For the moment, Saul was impressed by David's loyalty, and he went back home. Later, however, the manhunt continued.

Leader's Note 

Write on the board: "Stay true to your principles."

Elijah (*1 Kings 19:1-18; background: chapter 18*)

What was this person dealing with?
Elijah had won an amazing victory over the false prophets, calling down fire from heaven. But Queen Jezebel was now seeking his life, so he had to flee. Elijah was dealing with a mountaintop experience (literally!) one day, only to run for his life the next.

How did he or she deal with it?
Elijah let the emotions run their course. Hiding in a cave isn't always the best way to deal with stuff, but it might be okay for a while. Sometimes you need to take a break, camp out in your room for a night or two, pull away from other people. But then, like Elijah, let God call you out of the cave to see the way he works.

What was the result?
God gave Elijah work to do, and Elijah did it. (Sometimes that's the best way out of depression, to get involved with some important project.)

Leader's Note 

Write on the board: "Let your emotions run their course."

Esther (*Esther 4:11-16; background: Esther 3:8-9; result: Esther 8:7*)

What was this person dealing with?

A threat to her people. Esther was a queen in the Persian Empire, but she had no real power. It was even risky for her to approach the king without being sent for. But she learned of a plot to kill the Jews, and so she had a tough decision to make.

How did he or she deal with it?

Supported by the prayers of her people, Esther took a chance, a big chance, in alerting the king to Haman's plot.

What was the result?

The king put an end to the plot, punished the plotter, and rewarded Esther.

Leader's Note *Write on the board: "Risk doing the right thing."*

Daniel (*Daniel 6:3-23*)

What was this person dealing with?

New legislation that made it illegal to pray to anyone except the king.

How did he or she deal with it?

Daniel kept doing what he always did. He prayed to the Lord three times a day.

What was the result?

For his illegal praying, Daniel was thrown into a den of hungry lions, but God kept them from eating him. He emerged unharmed, and the king praised Daniel's God.

Leader's Note *Write on the board: "Continue good habits."*

So What?

I imagine you've got a lot of stuff to deal with right now. Maybe you're anxious about all your schoolwork, or you're depressed about some relationship, or you're confused about what to do with the rest of your life. Let's pin that down a little, and then we can talk about how to deal.

Turn your handout over and write three things. At the top write DEALING WITH . . . A third of the way down, write STRATEGY. Two-thirds down, write WHAT DOES THIS LOOK LIKE?

So now, back to the top. What are you dealing with? I'm going to run a few things by you. If that's what you're dealing with, write it down. You could write down two or three things if you want, whatever you're dealing with right now.

"Shredded Schedule" – just too much stuff to do.
"Brain Overload" – too much stuff to think about.
"Rocked Emotions" – feelings you don't know how to handle.
"Fried Friendships" – maybe people are just being weird right now.
"Spiritually Wasted" – God seems really far away.
"Other" – maybe there's something else the other categories don't include.

Repeat the list. **Leader's Note**

Now let's look at our strategies. I'm sure there are many, many options, but let's look at the eight things we gathered from today's Bible study.

Ask God for help . . . like Cain.
Wrestle with God . . . like Jacob.
Get others to help . . . like Moses.
Cling to God-honoring relationships . . . like Ruth.
Stay true to your principles . . . like David.
Let your emotions run their course . . . like Elijah.
Risk doing the right thing . . . like Esther.
Continue good habits . . . like Daniel.

As you look at the stuff you're dealing with, which of these strategies might work for you? They're all good ideas, of course, but can you find one of them that will specifically help you deal with your specific situation? Write that down on the middle part of your paper.

Now we need to get really specific. What does that look like? Sure, you want to "continue good habits," but *which* habits? In your specific case, how will you put this strategy into action?

Asking God for help. That's pretty basic. But have you done that? Sometimes we get the idea that we got ourselves into this mess, so we need to get out of it. That's not how God sees it. He wants to hear from you.

Wrestling with God. This is the odd one. My question is: Have you been avoiding God in this situation you're dealing with? Maybe you're even a little upset with him for letting it happen, so you're not on speaking terms right now. Well, why not take it to him and let him have it? Tell him exactly how you feel. Grab onto him and say, "I will not let you go unless you bless me." Then see what happens.

Getting others to help. Do you need to enlist help from your friends, or even your parents, to restructure your schedule? Sometimes we just take on too much, and we want to get it all done, but we can't. Moses had that same problem, and he found others to share the load.

Clinging to God-honoring relationships. Ruth wasn't sure how she was going to deal with everything, but she knew who she'd be dealing with – Naomi. Maybe you need to reconnect with a special friend, a brother or sister, or your parents. Sometimes solidifying that relationship can help put everything else into perspective.

Staying true to your principles. Sometimes our lives get complicated when we ignore basic stuff like helping others, pleasing God, using the gifts God has given. If you've got some tough decisions to make, or if you're in the midst of confusion, go back to those basic principles, and see if that sorts things out.

Let your emotions run their course. It's okay to cry sometimes. If you've lost something or someone important to you, you have the right to shut down for a while and be sad. It's okay to be angry sometimes, if you're careful about what you do with the anger. God gave you your emotions, so let them do what they need to do. Give yourself some "cave time" if you need it.

Risk doing the right thing. Sometimes we talk ourselves out of doing the right thing, because that's the scariest option. It's easier to go with the flow, to do what everyone expects, but maybe you need to take a chance on some radical action that will make God very happy. One bit of advice here. Esther got some good support from her cousin Mordecai, and it's good for you to seek the support of a wise friend or family member before doing anything crazy.

Continue good habits. When we have a lot to deal with, we can start neglecting some of the good habits that bring order to our lives – daily prayer, for instance, or going to church. Maybe even something like telling our parents we love them. Re-establish those habits and other things may fall into place.

Zero in on the strategy that you think you need, and find a specific way to do that. What habit? What principles? What risk? What relationship? Write down your plan.

Just Do It

One more question. What are you going to do about this *tomorrow*?

You've got the strategy. You know what it looks like. Now decide on an action step. What is something you can start doing tomorrow – or even later today? Write that at the very bottom of your worksheet.

As we close, I want to remind you that God knows what you're dealing with, and he's always ready to help you. Listen to his words from Psalm 46.

Leader's Note *Read Psalm 46 aloud or ask an expressive student to do so.*

06 fill your mind

Objectives

- Group members will learn from the book of Philippians about dealing with anxiety, depression, and difficult circumstances.
- They will consider how they can deal with anxious, depressing situations.

Bible Reference

Philippians.

Preparation

Go to www.BlueFishTV.com/Handouts and click Revolution Volume 1. Then click on the *Fill Your Mind* lesson to download "*Dr. Philippians*" handout and make copies for the whole class; index cards for the opening activity; chalkboard or equivalent; pens/pencils.

Startup

We're now going to play that game sensation – "What's worse?" I'm handing out index cards, and I want you to write down an activity you would not want to do. What's the worst thing that you could ever be forced to do? Eating roaches? Shaving gorillas? Smelling your brother's socks? Think *Fear Factor* here, and write something down. If you've got two or three ideas, grab an extra card.

Leader's Note

Gather the cards and go through a pair or two. "Which is worse: Eating roaches, or smelling your brother's socks?" But then stop and hand out more cards. Ideally these are of a different color or marked with different color.

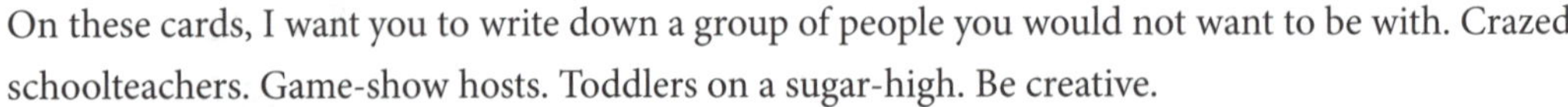

On these cards, I want you to write down a group of people you would not want to be with. Crazed schoolteachers. Game-show hosts. Toddlers on a sugar-high. Be creative.

Leader's Note *Gather these cards and keep the piles separate. Now you can play a couple rounds of "Double What's Worse?" Pull two cards from each pile, randomly matching the activity with the people-group. "Which is worse: Eating roaches with crazed schoolteachers, or joining with game-show hosts to smell your brother's socks?" After a few matchups, stop and hand out even more cards, preferably of a third color.*

For these cards, you have a choice. You could write down either a place you wouldn't want to be, a sound you wouldn't want to hear, or a weather condition that would make life miserable.

Leader's Note *Gather these cards and keep the three piles separate. Now you are entering the world of "Triple What's Worse?" Are you ready? Randomly connect three cards of different colors, and then match that triplet against another. "Which is worse: Shaving gorillas with crazed schoolteachers in a monsoon, or eating roaches with sugared-up toddlers while listening to German opera?" Run through this competition repeatedly, until the hilarity fades.*

I don't know if you ever go through situations quite that bad, but it probably feels like it. Lots of things in our lives can make us afraid or depressed or confused or just a little worried. How do you get through?

There's a Bible verse we'll be looking at a bit later, but it might apply here. In Philippians 4, the apostle Paul says, "I have learned to be content whatever the circumstances ... I have learned the secret of being content in any and every situation." Now I don't know if he ever played "Triple What's Worse?" but I'm sure he would have found a way to deal with those crazed schoolteachers or smelly socks [*whatever your game came up with*]. Let's find out more.

Bible Discovery

Turn to Philippians 1. Would someone read verses 3-6?

The apostle Paul is writing this letter. How does he feel about the Philippians? (He is thankful for them.)

What is he "confident" about? (That God began a good work in them and will keeping working in them.)

Take another look at verse 6. That's not just for the Philippians; it's for all of us. If we are Christians, God has begun a good work in us. We can be confident that he's going to keep working within us.

So if you're in one of those "What's Worse?" situations in your life, when you're feeling anxious, depressed, or confused, how does verse 6 help you out? (It can give you confidence that God is still with you, still working things out.)

Let's move ahead to verse 12. Would somebody read that?

"Something" happened to Paul. We'll find out more about that later. But, whatever it is, how does he feel about it now? (He thinks it has served to advance the gospel, so it's a good thing.)

Look at verse 13. What else do we learn about what happened to him? (He is in chains, so whatever happened, it got him arrested and imprisoned. But that's okay, he says, because all his guards have to hear him preach about Jesus. Talk about a captive audience! He's the captive, but they're the audience.)

Would someone read verses 14-17?

There's something else wrong in this situation. What is it? (There are some Christians who are Paul's enemies. They are taking advantage of his imprisonment to develop their own selfish ambition. They're trying to stir up trouble for him, trying to become famous by tearing him down.)

Take a look at verse 18. How did Paul respond to these rival preachers? (At least the gospel is being preached, he says. It's not about Paul; it's about Christ.)

What do you think about Paul's perspective here? Is he just trying to look at the bright side of everything, or is there something else in his thinking? (He is focused on the mission God gave him – sharing the message of Christ. As he sees it, it doesn't matter whether he has to endure imprisonment or insults, as long as the mission is accomplished.)

So when you're in a terrible situation, how could Paul's perspective help you? (Think about how God can use it to fulfill his purposes.)

Let's say you were falsely accused of something at school, and you're given a detention. Now you'd have every right to be mad about the false accusation, and you might worry about how this might affect your permanent record. Anxiety, anger, depression – all of that would be very normal. OR, you could think about how this detention puts you together with a group of people you don't normally hang out with. Maybe there's some way you could show them the love of Christ, the joy of Christ, or the truth of Christ.

Leader's Note

Divide into groups of 4-6. Distribute the "Dr. Philippians" handout. Give each group an assignment code: A, B, or C. Obviously, if you have more than three groups, you'll be doubling up on some assignments. Give them 10 minutes or so to study their assigned Scriptures and answer the questions, then bring them back together for discussion.

Philippians 1:21-24 (A)

What's the main point here? (Paul is comfortable with the thought that he might die soon. It's a win-win situation. If he lives, he gets to honor Christ with his earthly life. If he dies, he gets to enjoy being with Christ in heaven.)

How could this help someone get through tough circumstances? (Worst case: you die. But that's still a win for the believer. We know that Christ is with us in any situation, in life or death.)

Philippians 2:3-11 (B)

What's the main point here? (Jesus gave up his privileges in heaven to become a servant on earth. We should have that same attitude.)

How could this help someone get through tough circumstances? (It's not about you. It's not important how much glory or comfort or money you get. The important thing is to serve the Lord. Once that becomes your main goal, then you can trust the Lord to use any situation for his ultimate glory.)

Philippians 2:14-16 (C)

What's the main point here? (We need to keep a good attitude – without whining or bickering – because we want to shine for Christ within this wicked world.)

How could this help someone get through tough circumstances? (Our mission is to keep giving God glory.)

Philippians 3:7-8 (A)

What's the main point here? (Everything that Paul used to boast about is now just rubbish, compared to knowing Christ.)

How could this help someone get through tough circumstances? (It could give you a different perspective on what's important. A romantic breakup, a bad grade, not making the team – any of those could be painful, but none of what you've lost compares to knowing Christ.)

Philippians 3:12-14 (B)

What's the main point here? (Paul keeps moving forward, trying to please Jesus.)

How could this help someone get through tough circumstances? (We can put aside our past disappointments and plan how we'll live in the future.)

Philippians 4:2-3 (C)

What's the main point here? (Apparently Euodia and Syntyche were two women in the church who were fighting. Paul pleads with them to patch up their differences, and he asks other church members to help.)

How could this help someone get through tough circumstances? (Don't let your problems cause you to bicker with others, especially others in the church. We've all got more important work to do.)

Philippians 4:4 (B)

What's the main point here? (We should rejoice in all situations.)

How could this help someone get through tough circumstances? (No matter how bad the circumstances are, we can find joy in our relationship with the Lord.)

Philippians 4:6-7 (A)

What's the main point here? (Why worry when you can pray? Bring your concerns to the Lord and he will give you peace.)

How could this help someone get through tough circumstances? (We often forget this basic truth. The Lord stands ready to help. Worrying will not change the situation, but prayer can. Prayer also puts us in connection with God, giving us comfort, perspective, and direction.)

Philippians 4:8-9 (C)

What's the main point here? (There are many good things for us to fill our minds with. You could spend your day fretting about everything that can go wrong – or you could focus on what's true, noble, right, pure, lovely, admirable, excellent, and praiseworthy.)

How could this help someone get through tough circumstances? (We make things worse by worrying, by dwelling on insults we receive, by envisioning everything that could go wrong. By filling our minds with better stuff, we can transform our attitude.)

So What?

Let's all turn to Philippians 4:11. Apparently they had sent him a letter asking how he was doing. Now he thanks them for their concern. Somebody read verses 11-12.

What situations has Paul been in? (Good and bad, times of plenty and times of need.)

What's his attitude about all that? (Contentment.)

He talks about the "secret of being content." Based on everything we have read today, what do you think that secret is? (It seems to be a focus on what's really important. He wants to please Christ. He wants to fulfill his mission of preaching Christ. He feels he can trust Christ to help him do this important stuff. He doesn't need personal gain – in fact, that's just rubbish compared to Christ.)

Somebody read verse 13.

Whose strength is he talking about? (God's.)

As you see this verse in context, what's the "everything" he's talking about? Is he saying you can climb Mount Everest, run for president, or make a million dollars before you're 20? (Maybe, but probably not.)

This is not a blank check for the power to do anything you want to do. It's a promise of power for the things *He* wants you to do. Paul is talking about being content in any situation. You can get through anything, because God will give you strength.

I'm going to read you three different case studies. If this was a friend of yours expressing this problem, what verse from Philippians would you offer to help. I know there are a lot of helpful things you could say, but that's the rule of this game: just verses from Philippians.

Case Study A

I don't know when I'll get it all done. I've got two papers due on Friday, plus an exam, but I've got a different activity every night – band, youth group, the play, and tennis practice after school. But if I don't get good grades in those subjects, it hurts my class standing, and that might keep me from getting into the college I want, or at least getting the scholarship I need. But they also look at extra-curriculars, so I have to stay with all the other stuff, too. Honestly, I haven't been sleeping well, worrying about all the things I have to do. I really don't know how I'll get through it.

Now, what verses from Philippians might help this person? Give me a verse and tell me how it applies.

Several verses might work here. Philippians 4:6 urges us not to worry, but to pray, and the next verse speaks of God's peace that exceeds our understanding. Obviously, you need a lot of peace. Philippians 4:13 – "I can do everything through him" – could also help. But you might want to consider 3:7-8, in which Paul considers everything else (class standing? college? extracurricular?) "rubbish" compared to knowing Christ. Maybe Jesus would want you to drop some activities in order to follow his direction.

Case Study B

My boyfriend and I just broke up. Well, it was a week ago, and I've been crying most of the time since. It was a mutual decision, the right thing to do, but I've still been crying a lot. The thing is, I knew that we were going to spend our lives together. God had called both of us into inner-city ministry, and we were planning what college to attend, where to go to seminary, where we could do our internship, and all that. We weren't just a couple; we were a ministry team. But lately he was having second thoughts. And third thoughts and fourth thoughts. He wants to have a career in music. He wants to travel with this band of his. I think he's just chasing after worldly fame and fortune, but that's his choice. And that's kind of why we broke up. So now my whole future is up for grabs. All my dreams are dashed.

Now, what verses from Philippians might help this person?

Look at Philippians 3:13-14. Forget what is behind and keep pressing forward into the future God has for you. You might also find some joy in 4:4. And maybe this is the time to put aside your regrets and disappointments and look for the true, noble, right things of Philippians 4:8.

Case Study C

I'm not sure I want to be a Christian anymore. Oh, I believe in Jesus with all my heart. I love Christ; it's Christians I can't stand. We had this youth group planning meeting, and I made a few suggestions. Well, everybody was like, "We can't do that. That's so dumb." Or, "We tried that and it didn't work." I don't think they really understood what I was saying. A couple of times they even interrupted me with their own ideas, which weren't half as good as mine. So, anyway, I have a really bad feeling about Christianity now. I was starting to get excited about Jesus, but now I'm not so sure. If you're starting a monastery or something, and I can go off and follow Jesus on my own, I'm there. But if I have to spend a lot of time with these clowns, forget it.

What verses from Philippians might help this person?

The example of Jesus in Philippians 2:5-11 might help. Though he was Lord of all, he allowed himself to be not only interrupted but executed. In 2:14 (and 4:2) we're urged to avoid bickering and complaining. You may have been mistreated; sometimes Christians do that. But if we all see ourselves as servants, it will be harder to offend us. And maybe you good look for the "excellent" and "praiseworthy" things in this group (4:8).

Just Do It

Life can be crazy. You may be juggling a bunch of activities, along with school and relationships. Your mind may be crammed full of facts, ideas, news, gossip, worries, plans, and questions. And that can make you anxious. It can keep you from sleeping well. It can get you depressed. You might feel distracted or confused.

We've looked at Philippians 4:8 a couple of times today. On the surface, it seems like a nicey-nice verse. You know what I mean. "Think happy thoughts! Only nice things!" But it's far, far deeper than that.

Paul had a lot of rubbish going on in his life. Remember, he was in prison! He wasn't telling us to ignore reality. He was saying that you need to reach through all the rubbish and grab that gem of truth, of goodness, of rightness. You can fill your mind with anxiety, depression, or confusion – or you can find that wonderful thing that God gives you, that lesson, that plan, that pat on the back, that kick in the butt. Fill your mind with God's purposes, and you won't have room for anxiety or depression.

As we close, let me offer the prayer that Paul offers at the beginning of Philippians.

[*Read Philippians 1:9-11.*]

07 anger

Objectives

- Group members will learn from the video about anger – feeling it and dealing with it.
- In the lesson, they will review the ideas in the video and consider how they can handle their own anger.

Bible Reference

Psalms 4:4-5; Ephesians 4:26-27; James 1:19-20.

Preparation

Go to www.BlueFishTV.com/Handouts and click Revolution Volume 1. Then click on the *Anger* lesson to download "*Too Hot?*" handout and make copies for the whole class; set up TV/DVD player; *Anger* DVD; pens/pencils.

Startup

It really makes me mad when . . . drivers pull in front of me and then go, like, three miles an hour.

It really makes me mad when . . . celebrities talk on television like they know what's going on, when it's obvious they don't.

It really makes me mad when . . . my computer breaks down in the middle of an important project.

It really makes me mad when . . . I'm at a movie and right at the good part a cell phone rings in the row behind me, and then the person answers it and says, very loudly, "Guess where I am! I'm watching a MOVIE!"

How would you complete that sentence: "It really makes me mad when . . ."?

Leader's Note

Use your own examples to start things off, but you could certainly adapt the ones suggested here. You will set the tone with your examples, and you don't want it to get too heavy too soon. So keep it rather light, day-to-day frustrations rather than deep relationship issues or personal problems.

Showtime

Show *Anger* video

Re:view

We heard a couple of times that anger isn't necessarily a bad thing. Is that really true? How can that be? (The basic feeling of anger is a God-given emotion – a response to a situation that is unfair or threatening in some way. But anger can be dangerous. If we lose control, it can lead us into violence.)

Turn to Ephesians 4:26. Would someone read verses 26-27?

Does this tell us not to get angry? (No. In fact, it assumes we will.)

What does it tell us about dealing with anger? (First, do not let the anger lead you into sin. Control your behavior. Second, don't let anger fester. Resolve it before the day is done. Otherwise, you may give the devil a foothold in your life.)

How might the devil use anger as a foothold? What does that mean? (If you're angry with someone, you may plan ways to hurt them. If you harbor anger, you may develop a bad attitude, including hatred, pride, selfishness, or impatience.)

How can we resolve our anger? It's fine to say we shouldn't stay angry overnight, but how? How can we undo anger? (Ideally, you would go to the person and make peace. Maybe the offender has some excuse or explanation. Maybe you can offer forgiveness and it will be accepted. But that's not always possible, and sometimes those face to face confrontations just make matters worse. Yet Ephesians 4 doesn't make it sound too complicated. Whether or not the other person ever apologizes, you have the choice to stoke your anger or stop it.)

Turn to Psalm 4. Would someone read verses 4-5?

Sound familiar? Do these verses give us any clues about how to keep anger from festering day after day? (Don't go over and over all the things that made you mad. Quiet down. "Searching your heart" might even involve understanding that you're not perfect either. If somebody hurt you, maybe you've hurt them too. The "sacrifices of righteousness" are ways of getting yourself right with God. If someone has hurt you, offer your anger up to God and trust him to deal with it.)

In the video, they talked about two types of anger. Some are "exploders" and others are "imploders." What's the difference? (Exploders let the anger out, with violent words or actions. Imploders keep it bottled up inside.)

Is it better to be an exploder or an imploder? (Both can be bad. Exploders can be dangerous to others. Imploders can be dangerous to themselves. Imploders also store away their anger for a future time. "I don't get mad; I get even.")

One of the people interviewed said she felt "relieved" after she got angry. Have you ever felt that way? Why would anyone feel relieved after going on an angry tirade? (That's pretty common. Here's a gross example. If you're feeling sick to your stomach, the discomfort might get worse and worse until you puke. Then you feel relieved, because you've gotten rid of the problem. Except now someone has to clean it up. Same thing with anger.)

Doug Fields recommended three things we could do with our anger. Do you remember what they were? (Name It. Delay It. Learn from it.)

What does it mean to "name" your anger? What good does that do? (Sometimes you just get angrier and angrier until you forget what originally made you angry. If you name it, you can deal with it.)

Why is it a good idea to delay your anger? (It might keep you from doing something dumb. In the moment of anger, you want to hurt the person who has hurt you. You're not thinking about the consequences. You're just lashing out. If you wait a minute – "count to ten" – you can avoid doing things you'll regret later.)

What kind of things can you learn from your anger? (You can learn about yourself – how you respond to a challenge, what makes you angry, and what you really care about. Do you have certain emotional "hot buttons" you need to be careful about? How good are you at controlling your actions, or your words?)

Think about this. You probably don't get very angry in situations where you feel confident. If Shaquille O'Neal hears some fan yelling, "You don't know how to play basketball," he shrugs it off, because he knows he does. But if you're the third-string guard, and your teammates are yelling the same thing, that might make you mad.

This happens in romantic relationships all the time. A girl gets mad at her boyfriend for not calling her. It's not that she needs to talk to him every minute, but she's worried that he's not interested in her anymore. She's vulnerable in that area. If she names the anger and then delays her response so she can think about it first – maybe they both can learn a positive way to deal with that situation.

In the video, it was mentioned that some anger comes out in self-destructive behavior. Like what? What do people do to hurt themselves when they're angry? (Some throw themselves into drugs, drinking, or sex. Some pick fights or cut themselves. Some intentionally destroy relationships with the people closest to them. Say a teacher makes you mad; you might take it out on your parents – or vice versa. Anger spills. You want to be careful about how it messes up your life.)

What is self-control? What does it look like? Can you give me an example? (It's when you do the right thing rather than just following an impulse. With anger, it's when you get mad, you have a right to be mad, but you choose to do something positive rather than hurtful.)

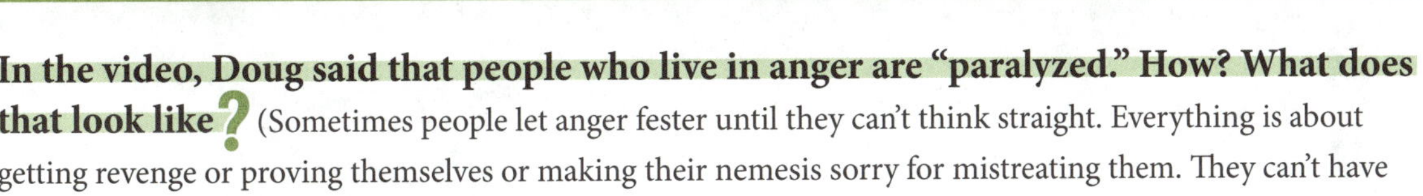

Leader's Note

Can you come up with an example of self-control in your own life, or something you've observed among these students?

In the video, Doug said that people who live in anger are "paralyzed." How? What does that look like? (Sometimes people let anger fester until they can't think straight. Everything is about getting revenge or proving themselves or making their nemesis sorry for mistreating them. They can't have honest relationships or accomplish anything valuable because it's all about the past.)

In order to get rid of your anger, it's important to forgive those who have hurt you, but how? What does that mean?

A lot of people have wrong ideas about forgiveness. Forgiveness is not excusing the person. It's *not* saying that whatever they did was okay. On the contrary, forgiveness says, "Hey, that's wrong, but I will not hold it against you." It helps when people ask you for forgiveness, but it's not necessary. You can forgive someone on your own – just by refusing to hold a grudge against them. Forgiveness means letting go of your right to get revenge. Forgiveness does not automatically make everything the way it was before.

For the Christian, forgiveness is based on the reality of being forgiven. We might get angry at someone who has wronged us, but then we must remember that we have done wrong things too. Sure, we have a right to be angry, just as God has a right to be angry with us. But God has forgiven us through Jesus, so we need to extend forgiveness to others.

Just Do It

Leader's Note

Distribute the "Too Hot? handout.

Here are several helpful ideas you could try out. You don't have to fill out every section. It's up to you. I'll give you a few minutes now to work through this sheet on your own, but you could also take it home and work on it some more.

Leader's Note

Give them 6-10 minutes to work on this. Then pull them back together for wrap-up and closing prayer.

[*Read James 1:19-20.*]
Anger comes through our lives and it has its purposes, but you don't want to get stuck there, because it doesn't really help you live a righteous life. So be quick to listen and slow to speak. It's not all about you and your rights. Look out for the interests of others. That will help to make you "slow to become angry."

08 soul on fire

Objectives

- Group members will learn how Jesus dealt with anger and anger-causing situations.
- They will consider how they can deal with such situations in their own lives.

Bible Reference

John 2:1-5,13-16; Matthew 4:8-10; 16:5-12,21-23; 17:14-21; 23:13-14,23-24; Mark 6:1-6; 11:12-14; Luke 13:31-35; 23:32-43

Preparation

Go to www.BlueFishTV.com/Handouts and click Revolution Volume 1. Then click on the *Soul on Fire* lesson to download "*HWJF?*" handout and make copies for the whole class; whipped cream and a supply of colorful, loopy, doughnut-shaped breakfast cereal for the opening activity; optional prize for opening activity (see Leader's Note below) pens/pencils.

Startup

We'll begin today with a competition involving skill and strategy, pitting three teams in against one another in a fierce display of physical and mental dexterity. No, we're not talking about chess, or even Texas Hold'em, but a little game we call "Loopyface."

We need three pairs of people to play this game. One person from each team will stand here, throwing (*cereal brand*) to his or her partner, who will stand here (*about three feet away*). The winning team will be the one that catches the most loops. But wait! The receiver may not use his or her hands to catch the loops. They must use only their face to catch the loops. How will they do that? Well, they're going to smear whipped cream on their faces before they start. We'll give you 47 seconds to toss the loops, and then we'll stop and count. There will be a cash prize for the winners.

*Count up the winners and announce the winning team. Then give a dollar to one member of the third-place team. (You could use another prize, of course – a CD or book or T-shirt – but it needs to be something of real value.) You could just say, "I like the way this person played the game," or something like that. Then move on with the session and see how long you can go before they start grumbling. Look for the *** symbol below to respond to the grumbling.*

Bible Discovery

Today we'll be looking at the life of Jesus and some of his emotions. We're used to thinking of Jesus as the divine Son of God, but sometimes we forget that he was also human. That means he experienced the same emotions we feel, but we know he handled them without sin. He got sad, he got frustrated, he had times when he needed to get away from it all, and he even got angry. Turn to John 2. Would someone read verses 1-3?

Where was Jesus? (At a wedding.)

What did Jesus' mother say to him? (They have no more wine.)

What do you think she wanted him to do about it? (A miracle?)

It certainly seems that Mary was nudging Jesus into his first miracle. Obviously she knew his identity as the Son of God, and maybe she sensed that this would be the right time for him to go public. Let's see how Jesus responded. Somebody read verses 4-5.

How did Jesus respond to his mother's request? (I'm not ready yet.)

Have you ever responded to your parents like that? (It's a safe guess that most kids have said, "It's not my job," "I'll get to it later," or something like that.)

So how would you describe Jesus' feelings when he said that? Was he annoyed, angry, impatient, or what?

We could interpret these words in many ways. "Dear woman" is not a nasty term, but it's not tender either. At face value, these words sound like a conflict, the kind of thing teens and parents have every day. There's no reason to scour the conflict out of it. Jesus was now an adult, almost 30, so he was not sassing his mom. And we don't know how Mary made the request. We don't want to disrespect either Mary or Jesus, but conflicts like this arise in all families.

How do you feel when your parents tell you to do things? How about when they just point out a need? "The grass is growing long." "The table needs to be set." (We don't like it when we have to do chores. But there's also an issue of independence. Increasingly, as they grow, teens make more of their own decisions, but they still need to obey their parents. That's why parents sometimes point out a need, as Mary did, allowing a teenager to make the choice to meet that need.)

Jesus said his "time" had not yet come. What did he mean? (The time to begin his ministry as a public preacher, healer, and miracle worker.)

When did the time come? (Apparently a few minutes later.)

If you glance over the next few verses, you'll see that Jesus did just what Mary wanted. He worked a miracle to turn water into wine. This was his first miracle, and it launched his ministry.

We can wonder a lot about Jesus' feelings in this story, but what did he DO? (He did what Mary wanted. He performed a miracle to provide wine.)

When we're annoyed at someone who's telling us what to do, we often do the exact opposite. We assert our independence and go off in our own direction, even if the annoying person was right. Sometimes we'll do the wrong thing – even if we know it's wrong – just to prove that we can do what we want.

We don't know that Jesus was annoyed, but from what he said, that's a possibility. But he didn't let his feelings keep him from doing the right thing. Skip down to verse 13. Would someone read John 2:13-16?

What was the situation that got Jesus upset? (People were selling animals and exchanging money in the Temple courts.)

Why do you think animals were being sold? (People were supposed to bring animals to the Temple to be sacrificed. If people were traveling a long way, it was easier to buy an animal at the Temple.)

At this time, the Romans had taken over Israel, along with much of the world, and so people used Roman money in everyday life. But the religious leaders considered the Romans to be dirty and godless, so it would be wrong to use Roman money in the holy Temple of God. So, when people came to buy their sacrifices at the Temple, they had to exchange their "dirty" Roman money for "holy" Temple shekels. The problem was, this became a big racket. The moneychangers would hike up the price of the Temple money and they'd pocket the profits.

So what was Jesus angry about? (He talks about how they've turned God's house into a market. But it's not just that they were selling stuff; it's that they were cheating people in order to make money. And who were they cheating? The people who came to worship God! That's not right.)

***

Oh, are you still upset about the prizes? Why? (It isn't fair. The prize was promised to the winning team, but given to someone on the losing team!)

So I understand why the winners are upset, but what about the rest of you? I didn't hurt you at all. Why should you be bothered? (Because it still isn't right. A promise was made.)

Set it right by awarding prizes (possibly even better ones) to the winners.

When things aren't right, we get angry. It upsets us when we're treated unfairly, but sometimes we also respond to unfairness toward others. That's what Jesus was dealing with here. Not only was he upset about the desecration of God's house, but he also opposed the unfair treatment of worshipers.

In this situation with the moneychangers, how did Jesus show his anger? (He made a whip and drove the animals out of the area. He overturned the tables of the moneychangers.)

Do you think he hurt people or damaged property? (There's no indication that he whipped any *people* or that he physically attacked anyone. That wouldn't be Jesus' style. Jesus chased away animals that belonged to the sellers and he messed up the money tables. This action would be considered vandalism.)

So is vandalism okay if it's for a good cause? (No. Remember that Jesus is the Son of God, so he gets away with a lot of stuff we don't.)

Distribute the "HWJF?" handout and divide into groups of 4-6. Give each group one of the three assignments—A, B, or C. Have them read the assigned passages and discuss answers to the questions. After 8-10 minutes, draw the groups back together to talk about their responses.

Matthew 4:8-10 (A)

What situation could have upset Jesus? (The devil was tempting him. Jesus might have been upset by the devil's arrogance in claiming to have possession of "all the kingdoms of the world" – or at the mere thought of worshiping anyone but his Father God.)

How would you describe Jesus' feelings in this situation? (Hungry. Embattled. Spiritually tuned in. It's not clear that Jesus was angry, but there's probably a sense that "Enough is enough!")

What did Jesus do with these feelings? (He yelled at the devil: *Away from me!*)

Why do you think he responded this way? (It was time to end this. He had passed the test. He was ready to move on with his ministry.)

Matthew 16:5-12 (A)

What situation could have upset Jesus? (The disciples were dense. He had used picture-language to describe the Pharisees' teachings and the disciples had totally missed the point.)

How would you describe Jesus' feelings in this situation? (Disappointed. Frustrated. *Don't you get it yet?*)

What did Jesus do with these feelings? (He scolded his disciples.)

Why do you think he responded this way? (He had to challenge them to step up to a new level.)

Matthew 16:21-23 (C)

What situation could have upset Jesus? Peter was trying to talk him out of going to the cross.

How would you describe Jesus' feelings in this situation? Disappointed in Peter and bothered by this. Peter had just experienced a wonderful moment of truth, and now this.

What did Jesus do with these feelings? (He yelled at Peter, calling him "Satan.")

Why do you think he responded this way? (The cross was the whole point of his mission. Peter was delivering the same temptation Jesus had received in the desert. It was difficult for Jesus to keep pressing on toward the cross, and now even his star disciple was sabotaging him.)

Matthew 17:14-21 (B)

What situation could have upset Jesus? (The disciples could not heal a boy.)

How would you describe Jesus' feelings in this situation? (Disappointed? Impatient? Even after all his instruction, the disciples weren't practicing faith.)

What did Jesus do with these feelings? (He scolded his disciples for their lack of faith.)

Why do you think he responded this way? (He had been pouring his life into these guys, and they were slow learners. That's frustrating. But sometimes teachers scold to get attention. Maybe this tirade of Jesus was more of an effort to get an important point across in a way the disciples would get.)

Matthew 23:13-14,23-24 (B)

What situation could have upset Jesus? (The Pharisees were in charge of the religious scene, making it tough for ordinary people to worship God. They were enforcing details of the law, but missing the main point.)

How would you describe Jesus' feelings in this situation? (He was angry, on behalf of the people being shut out of God's kingdom.)

What did Jesus do with these feelings? (In this entire chapter, Jesus lets the Pharisees have it, with a blistering verbal attack.)

Why do you think he responded this way? (He needed to expose the Pharisees as the frauds they were. Filled with God's concern for the outsiders, he needed to make it clear that these ultimate insiders, the Pharisees, were NOT God's favorites.)

Mark 6:1-6 (A)

What situation could have upset Jesus? (In his home town, people weren't taking him seriously.)

How would you describe Jesus' feelings in this situation? (Hurt. Insulted. Frustrated, because he wanted to work miracles there, but they lacked the faith.)

What did Jesus do with these feelings? (He made a witty remark about prophets being ignored at home, and he just wouldn't do many miracles there.)

Why do you think he responded this way? (These were people he grew up with. He loved them. It would be natural for him to feel personally rejected, but he also wanted them to experience his miraculous healing power – yet they weren't buying it.)

Mark 11:12-14 (C)

What situation could have upset Jesus? (He wanted fruit from a fig tree. It wasn't there.)

How would you describe Jesus' feelings in this situation? (Hungry. Frustrated.)

What did Jesus do with these feelings? (He cursed the fig tree, so it wouldn't bear fruit again.)

Why do you think he responded this way? (This is a strange story. On the surface, it sounds selfish: "I want fruit, I can't get fruit, so no one will get fruit!")

But that doesn't sound like the Jesus we know – which makes us think it's a lesson of some kind. But what could he be teaching here?

In the Old Testament, the fig tree is sometimes used as a symbol for the nation of Israel. Was Israel not bearing the fruit God wanted? John the Baptist once challenged the Jewish leaders to "produce the fruit of repentance." Was Jesus looking for the Jewish leaders to open their hearts to God (and to him)? At other times Jesus was frustrated because a lack of faith kept him from doing the miracles he wanted to do. Maybe this is a picture of that frustration.

Luke 13:31-35 (B)

What situation could have upset Jesus? (He was threatened by King Herod.)

How would you describe Jesus' feelings in this situation? (He was challenged. And he was taking the challenge.)

What did Jesus do with these feelings? (He made a defiant statement of determination.)

Why do you think he responded this way? (He had work to do, and he was going to do it.)

Luke 23:32-43 (C)

What situation could have upset Jesus? (He was being crucified, and yet he was being mocked by passersby, and even by those who were crucified with him.)

How would you describe Jesus' feelings in this situation? (Amazingly, though he must have been in great pain, he seems to be full of love.)

What did Jesus do with these feelings? (He offered forgiveness to his killers and acceptance to the thief.)

Why do you think he responded this way? (Love was the reason he had done all of this. He had marched to the cross out of love for sinful people. He couldn't stop then.

So What?

What do we do with all of this? Obviously, Jesus faced a lot of bothersome situations, just as we do. He had a range of responses.

How did he respond when he was being tempted? (Strong words – "Away from me!" He resisted the temptation.)

How did he respond when he was personally threatened or insulted? (He sort of shrugged it off and kept doing his thing. Even on the cross, he kept loving.)

How did he respond when the disciples weren't getting it? (He used words to show his disappointment. Sometimes it sounds like scolding, but maybe he needed the strong words to get through to them.)

How did he respond when powerful people were keeping others from worshiping God? (He sometimes got violent in speech and actions.)

There are two parts to anger, the getting and the giving. You can control how angry you get, if you change your attitude about how much you deserve. If you see yourself as a servant, that can tone down your angry feelings.

The second part of anger is the giving, or the showing. You always have a choice about how you show the anger you're feeling. Will you say something helpful or say something hurtful? Will you try to hurt someone physically or do some damage to someone's property – or will you sink that energy into your mission of loving people and bringing them closer to God? You have choices to make, and God has the power to help you follow through on those choices.

Just Do It

Have you ever heard of the "Jesus Prayer?" This is a simple sentence that some people memorize and repeat throughout the day: "Lord Jesus, have mercy on me, a sinner."

If you have a problem with anger, you might try a variation on that theme. Memorize a sentence-prayer to say at those times when you start to feel your blood boil.

Here's a suggestion. Write this on the back of your handout. "I am Your servant. Let me be upset only by the things that upset You."

You can tinker with the wording to make it your own, but please try it out. It's like counting to ten. A simple prayer like this might give you perspective and control in upsetting situations.

09 doubt

Objectives

- Group members will learn from the video about the questions of their own hearts, and those of others.
- In the lesson, they will review the ideas in the video and consider how those questions might be answered.

Bible Reference

Matthew 11:2-6; Colossians 1:27; 1 Peter 2:12-23.

Preparation

Go to www.BlueFishTV.com/Handouts and click Revolution Volume 1. Then click on the *Doubt* lesson to download "*Q & A*" handout and make copies for the whole class; set up TV/DVD player; *Doubt* DVD; pens/pencils.

Startup

As we begin today, I have a simple question for you. I want you to think of a question you have asked or answered in the last 24 hours. What was that question? How was it answered?

Leader's Note

If no one can think of anything, suggest, "How are you?" or "What's going on?" It's just an icebreaker.

Why was the question asked? (Usually it's a simple desire for info, but not always.)

Was the asker satisfied with the answer? If not, why not?

Did the question really need an answer? Did it need an *honest* answer? ("How are you?" usually doesn't.)

Did the question-and-answer lead to any change in the relationship? Like what? (Say a guy asks a girl if she'll join him on a first date. Yes or no, that can change a relationship. Say your parents ask where you were at 11 pm last night, or they ask if you'll do a chore and you say no.)

Today we're talking about questions. You may have questions about your own faith. Or people around you might have questions about what you believe or how you live. How do you deal with those questions?

Showtime

Show *Doubt* video

Re:view

The video started with the guys from Grits. One of them said, "It is not our goal to market Christ. It's our goal to be like Christ and to live the life of Christ and allow that to impact the lives of those around us."

In what ways do Christians try to "market" Christ? (We portray Jesus as the fixer of all problems, the answer to every need. And he does offer amazing healing, as well as joy and fulfillment, but he also asks for our commitment.)

How did this band suggest we impact others? (By simply living the life of Christ – honestly being the people God has made us to be.)

Sometimes we try to tell those around us that we have all the answers for them, when the truth is, we don't even have all the answers for ourselves. Do you think your own doubts make it difficult for you to share your faith with others? (Sure, but sometimes it's even more effective when someone honestly shares their questions as well as their beliefs.)

Doug Fields said, "If I could understand everything there is to know about God, he wouldn't be God." What did he mean by that? Do you agree? (God is beyond us. He says, "My thoughts are higher than your thoughts" – Isaiah 55:9. If we could completely figure him out, then our thoughts would be just as high as his. We need a God who knows more; otherwise, how would he be able to help us?)

Turn to Matthew 11. Would someone read verses 2-3?

This is John the Baptist asking the question. He was the preacher who led a big revival and then he pointed to Jesus and said, "There's the one you should follow." But what is he asking now? (Are you the promised Messiah, or should we keep looking for someone else?)

Why do you think he was wondering about this? (Well, his doubts might have had something to do with the fact that he was in prison. He might have been depressed or even angry with God for letting things get to that point. He was in prison for speaking out boldly against sin, and yet Jesus seemed to be meandering around the country. Why wasn't Jesus making his move?)

In verses 4-6, how does Jesus answer John's doubts? (By referring to the things he was doing. He wasn't meandering aimlessly. He was bringing healing to the people, preaching good news, releasing people from spiritual captivity. This might not have been exactly the kind of Messiah that John wanted, but it was what God had promised.)

If a great preacher like John the Baptist had doubts about Jesus, so can you. It's natural to have questions, and you shouldn't feel guilty about not being 100% positive all the time. But what did John do with his questions? He took them to Jesus. And chances are, Jesus will give you the same answer. He might not be doing all the miracles you ask for, but he is transforming people's lives. Open your eyes and see.

We've been talking about your own questions and doubts. But how do you share your faith experience with your friends? There was an interesting question in the middle of the video: What do you do when people say, "*Christianity is fine for you, but leave me out of it. I don't need to hear your good news*"?

How would you answer that? How do you get your faith across to people who aren't attacking you – they just want nothing to do with Christianity?

It's a tough challenge. The Bible says we should "be ready to give an answer for the hope we have" (1 Peter 3:15), but what do you do when no one's asking? That same verse says we should speak with "gentleness and respect." You don't want to be screaming at people or disrespecting them.

This will sound weird, but let me ask you: Has there been an amazing CD, a great movie or an unbelievable food you have experienced lately? Not just good, I mean fantastic.

Have you told anyone else about that experience? Why? (You probably have, because you wanted to share something great with the people you care about.)

That same thing happens when we tell people about Jesus. We're not trying to carve notches in our belt so we get the Witnessing Prize in heaven someday. We have an awesome relationship with a stupendous Savior, and we just have to tell that to the people we care about.

Do you remember seeing Matt and Cody at the end of the video? How did Matt become a Christian? (His girlfriend kept talking about Jesus, until he finally agreed to go to church.)

Why do you think she did that? (Because she cared about him, and she wanted to share with him this important part of her life.)

People may ask you questions that you can't answer. Or they may challenge the answers you give. That's okay. Just talk about what you know. Is Jesus real in your life? Has he changed you at all? Then talk honestly and openly about that.

Just Do It

Leader's Note *Distribute the "Q & A" handout.*

Here are some quotes we heard from different kids in the video. My question for you is: How would you respond? If this were a friend of yours saying this, what would you say to them? Let's break up into groups of 4-5 and discuss it.

Leader's Note *Give them 5-6 minutes to work on this. Then pull them back together to discuss it.*

A **I do get angry with God sometimes just because sometimes he doesn't answer my prayers how I want them to be answered. And sometimes I feel like he's not even there.**

He's there. Sometimes you have to wait a while, sit quietly, before you sense him. "Be still, and know that I am God," he said (Psalms 46:10). He doesn't always do what we want him to do, but he does what's best for us. Face it, if your folks gave you cotton candy every time you asked for it, you wouldn't be very healthy today. It's okay to be angry with God, but tell him about it.

B **I have questioned whether Jesus dying on the cross for us was real, because it's just such an unbelievable story. A lot of people make up stories that we all believe are true but they aren't. So it makes me wonder: what if he didn't really die for us? And what if our religion isn't true?**

People do make up stories, which is why we need to look at the evidence. There is great evidence for the death and resurrection of Jesus. We all have those moments of worrying that it might be false, but keep coming back to the basics. And what makes the story of Jesus "unbelievable?" Is it the idea that people just don't rise from the dead? Well, that's what makes it a miracle – the fact that it doesn't happen all the time. If we believe in a powerful God, doesn't it make sense that he would do this one miraculous thing to provide salvation to the world?

C **After all the things I've done, it makes me think, What if I died today? I won't be able to go to heaven. I would do anything to go back and change that, doing all that stuff. Not drinking or smoking or having sex.**

There's one way to get into heaven, and it's not by living a good life. It involves coming humbly to Jesus and saying, "Please forgive me." You have the humble part already. You are sorry for your sin. If you haven't already, just pray to Jesus and ask him to forgive you. He will. That is your ticket to heaven. He will also transform your life, and maybe he's already doing that. You can't undo your past, but he can give you an amazing future.

When I got older I realized that the world is not everything it's cracked up to be. It's not perfect. And people are mean. And that's when I starting to question God. I was like, "Well, if he loved me, and he loved the world as much as he says he does, then why on earth would he make people as mean as they are?"

That's a question many people have grappled with. The answer rests in the idea of Freedom. God gave us the freedom to choose right or wrong, good or bad. We can choose to follow him or run away. As a result, some people (including us) make bad choices. Some people (including us, sometimes) choose to be mean. He didn't make us mean, but he gave us the freedom to choose meanness, or love.

He started making fun of me. He was, like, "Jesus? Why in the heck do you even like this guy? It's stupid!" He kept calling me a hypocrite and all that sort of thing. . . . I tried to explain to him who Jesus was, but it really didn't work.

Some people just don't get it. And they'll give you a hard time for what you believe. You might be tempted to fight back. If he insults you, you'll want to insult him. If he belittles your beliefs, you'll want to belittle his. But that's not the way Jesus wants us to live.

Let me read you some verses from 1 Peter 2. Peter was living in a world where it was tough to be a Christian – kind of like ours. Here's what he says about that.

Leader's Note

The verses are: I Peter 2:12, 15, 17, 20-21, 23 New International Version. If you like another translation, it would help to write the specific verses out in advance or mark them in your Bible.

"Live such good lives among the pagans that, though they accuse you of doing wrong, they may see your good deeds and glorify God on the day he visits us. . . . For it is God's will that by doing good you should silence the ignorant talk of foolish men. . . . Show proper respect to everyone. . . .How is it to your credit if you receive a beating for doing wrong and endure it? But if you suffer for doing good and you endure it, this is commendable before God."

So why are people giving you a hard time? Because you're sharing your faith, or because you're obnoxious about it? Peter says, "if you suffer *for doing good* and you endure it, this is commendable before God."

"To this you were called, because Christ suffered for you, leaving you an example, that you should follow in his steps. . . . When they hurled their insults at him, he did not retaliate; when he suffered, he made no threats. Instead, he entrusted himself to him who judges justly."

Let me close with this thought. You probably have some questions about your faith. And maybe your friends are asking you questions. Yes, there are some answers, and we can talk about those in future lessons. But it's not about having the right answer all the time. It's about having a relationship with Jesus Christ.

10 answer dance

Objectives

- Group members will learn about biblical characters who defended their faith in difficult environments.
- They will consider how they can be true to their faith in their own world.

Bible Reference

Judges 6-8; 1 Peter 2:11-12; 3:15-17; 5:6-9.

Preparation

Go to www.BlueFishTV.com/Handouts and click Revolution Volume 1. Then click on the *Answer Dance* lesson to download "*Ministry of Defense*" handout and make copies for the whole class; also download "*Answer Gal*" sketch and make 8 copies; 8 (or optional 4) actors to do the "*Answer Gal*" opening sketch; pens/pencils.

Startup

Leader's Note *After welcoming the group, introduce the opening sketch, "Answer Gal." This could be a case where you prepare the Answer Gal and boyfriend in advance, but choose 6 callers from the group to sight-read the script. Or have one or two skilled actors provide the voices for all 6 callers.*

[*After the sketch*] **Have you ever had to deal with questions like that – about creation or hypocrites or narrow-mindedness?**

Do you think the Answer Gal gave good answers?

The callers might have felt frustrated, as if the Answer Gal wasn't really listening to them. Sometimes as we interact with people who are questioning our faith, we can give the right answers in the wrong way. We need to respond with courtesy and love.

We saw a character who had all the answers about God, but seemed clueless in her personal life. Which do you think is more important?

Do you think the difficulties in her personal life would hurt her credibility? Would people have a hard time trusting her answers?

Both sides are important. We should be ready to give answers, but we should also demonstrate the truth of God in our lives. That doesn't mean we live perfect lives. In the case of the Answer Gal, she had to show humility, "putting down her pride" and maybe apologizing to her boyfriend. That personal authenticity would go a long way toward establishing her credibility. If you're hiding the truth about your faults, people may assume you're not interested in the truth of your answers.

Bible Discovery

Take your Bibles and turn to the book of Avengers, chapter 6. Oh, I'm sorry – you probably know this as the book of Judges, but the fact is, the word "Judges" isn't the best translation. It's not about people with gavels; it's about people with swords. They're called Judges because they fought to bring about God's Justice. So you might call them the Avengers.

What do we find in these stories? We find the Israelites threatened by some foreign army, and we find God raising up a champion to save the people. We find Gideon, Samson, Deborah, and some others stepping up to defeat the enemy and bring the people back to God. Today we'll be learning about Gideon.

Take a look at Judges 6:1-6. Who's the enemy this time? (The Midianites.)

What were the Midianites doing? (Swarming in and ruining the crops, forcing the Israelites to live in caves.)

How many of them were there? (Too many to count.)

So this was a pretty bleak situation. How did they get into this mess? (Verse 1 tells us they "did evil in the eyes of the Lord.")

This is the pattern throughout the book of Judges, and throughout the Old Testament. When the people turn away from God, he allows enemies to dominate them. When things get terrible, what do the Israelites do? Somebody read verse 6 out loud.

What did the people do? (They cried out to the Lord for help.)

So they cry for help and God saves them, and they worship God for a while. But over time they drift away again, and the whole cycle starts again. Aren't you glad we never do stuff like that? Obviously we're too smart to fall into that cycle, right?

Well, maybe not. Have you ever experienced that cycle – praying for help in bad times but ignoring God in the good times? Tell me about it.

Leader's Note *They may or may not have their own stories to tell. If not, just move on. Or you might have a story of your own to tell.*

Let's pick up the story in verse 11. Who comes to visit Gideon? (The angel of the Lord.)

Sometimes in the Bible angels appear in shining bright light. Other times they just look like ordinary guys. Apparently this one was wearing the ordinary-guy outfit. He comes and sits down under a tree to talk to Gideon.

What was Gideon doing? (Threshing grain in a winepress.)

The way they used to thresh grain was to take it to a hilltop and spread it out. Then they'd roll a heavy weight over the grain to crush it, and then they'd take a pitchfork and toss it up in the air. The husks would blow away in the breeze. The grain would fall straight down.

But Gideon wasn't threshing on a hilltop. Why not? (Because the Midianites might see him and steal the grain.)

He was threshing grain in a winepress, which was sort of like a bathtub. It's like playing baseball in a kitchen. You can do it, but not very well. Now would someone read verses 12-13?

What did the angel call Gideon? ("Mighty warrior.")

"The Lord is with you" was a pretty common greeting, like "How are you?" But how did Gideon respond? (With a ton of questions.)

How would you describe Gideon's state of mind? (Cynical? Depressed? Angry?)

Would someone read verses 14-16?

What does the Lord ask Gideon (through this angel)? (To save his people.)

How does Gideon respond? (Who me? I can't do it. I'm nobody.)

How does the Lord answer Gideon's objection? ("I will be with you.")

What kind of answer is that? Does that really resolve Gideon's problem? (Yes! Gideon's not going to do this in his own power. It's God's power that will win the victory.)

Today we're talking about defending our faith. Not that we're going to take swords and bash some heads, but we may have some moments of confrontation. There might be times when God will ask you to step forward and stand up for his truth.

Like Gideon, you might have a couple of problems. First, you might have some questions yourself. *What's going on? Why does God let bad stuff happen?* Your questions don't disqualify you. You don't need to have all the answers, or even pretend to. Be honest about what you know and what you don't know.

The second issue is this: "Who am I to stand up for God? I'm nobody. I'll just keep quiet and leave the speaking to the experts." And God's response is the same one he gave Gideon: "I will be with you." It's not your power or even your expertise that will convey God's truth to your world; it's Christ in you.

Let's get back to Gideon. As chapter 7 begins, he has gathered an army to face the Midianites. But the Lord has an interesting request. Somebody read verses 2-3.

As the Lord saw it, what was the problem? (Gideon had too many men.)

Yes, that's right. They were facing an army too numerous to count, hundreds of thousands of Midianites, and they manage to scrape together about thirty thousand men. But God says, "You have too many. If anyone's nervous about this, they can go home."

Why did God want a smaller army? (So that the Israelites would not boast that they had won the victory on their own. With a smaller army, it would be clear that it was God's power at work in them.)

So they cut the army down from 32,000 to 10,000, but the Lord has another request. Somebody read verses 4-7.

How many soldiers do they have now? (Only 300.)

Don't look for any great significance in how they drink the water. It was just God's way of cutting down the numbers. And now comes the good part. In the middle of the night, Gideon leads this band of 300 to the Midianite camp. Somebody pick up the story by reading verses 16-19.

What did Gideon's soldiers have in their hands? (Each had a torch, covered by a pitcher, and a trumpet in the other hand.)

What did they do on Gideon's command? (They broke the pitchers and blew the trumpets and shouted.)

If you were a Midianite, in that crowded camp, what would this experience be like for you? (In the middle of a dark night, you'd suddenly see the sky light up with 300 torches, and then you'd hear 300 trumpets sounding, and a shout. Rising from sleep, you'd grab a sword and swing it.)

Check out verse 21. The Midianites ran off, "crying as they went." It was a stunning victory for Gideon and the Israelites. They won, not because they had a stronger army, but because they were guided by a clever and creative God.

Now, what happens when you are called to defend your faith? Maybe some science teacher is suggesting that it's ignorant to believe in God. Or maybe some classmates are making fun of Christians. Or maybe a friend has some deep questions about God. You might think that you need to out-argue, out-fox, and out-shout everybody. Prove every point! Show them who's ignorant!

But maybe that's not God's way. Listen to him. Let his creative love guide you. Sometimes you'll need to do some research and have some answers. But other times it will be enough to say, "God is a reality in my life. I can't answer every objection you have, but I know God loves me, and he loves you too." You will not win these arguments in your own power. You have to do it God's way.

There's one more little Gideon story we should read. Turn to Judges 8:22. Someone read verses 22-23.

What did the people want to do for Gideon? (They want to make him king.)

How did he respond? (No, no. Only the Lord is king.)

Was that a good answer? (Absolutely. It's nice to see that Gideon wasn't grabbing personal power.)

But there's a little more to the story. Look at verse 24.

What did Gideon ask for? (Gold earrings that they had captured from the enemy.)

If you look at verse 27, you find Gideon using this gold to make an *ephod* [EE-fod], which was a breastplate worn by the priests. It was a holy garment, which was supposed to be used in the worship of God. But instead, he set it up as an idol in his home town, and people started worshiping *that*!

It says this became a "snare" to Gideon and his family – a trap. How would this experience entrap Gideon? (It was like idolatry, worshiping an object. It would lead them away from God. But it's also possible that this wasn't intended as an idol, but as a testament to Gideon's great righteousness. Hey, look how good Gideon is! He wins a great victory, and he's too humble to become king. Instead he offers this holy breastplate to God. What a righteous guy he is! That would play into Gideon's pride, and soon he would start thinking that he had won the victory on his own.)

Here's another important lesson. It's not about you. As you step up to defend the Christian faith, it's not about how righteous you are, how smart you are, or even how cool you are. It's about God's truth. When you set yourself up as an object of worship, you completely miss the point. That's a trap. Stay out of it.

So What?

When we talk about "defending our faith," what does that mean to you? How have you had to defend your faith? (Sometimes it happens in the form of sincere questions; other times it's criticism. People might say it's foolish to believe, or that they've grown beyond such childish ideas. But sometimes they really want to understand some part of the Bible that's giving them trouble.)

When people have objections to Christianity, where do you think that comes from, their mind or their heart? Are they having a hard time understanding or a hard time accepting? (There are some scientifically minded folks who just don't accept Christianity mentally. How could one obscure preacher from a little country 2,000 years ago die for the sins of the world and then come back to life? It makes no sense to them. But other people are operating from a heart-level. Maybe they've been hurt and they're punishing God by not believing. Maybe they want to live a wild and free life, with none of the moral restrictions of Christianity. Maybe they don't like the Christians they know.)

What difference would that make – mind or heart – in how you talk with them? (If someone has mental objections, you can engage in a reasonable debate – and you'd better do your homework. But if the objections are coming from the heart, you could win the debate and still lose the soul. In that case, it might be better to listen, to empathize, and to love.)

It might help to come up with some principles that will help us defend our faith with those around us. We've already been learning from Gideon. Maybe we can distill some principles from his story.

But there's another part of the Bible we ought to look at. The book of 1 Peter was written to Christians living in a secular society. In Gideon's day, the Midianites were in charge. In Peter's, it was the Romans. In this little New Testament letter, he gives practical advice on how to live for Christ in a world that doesn't agree with you.

As you work on this handout in your groups, you'll be asked to look at some passages from 1 Peter and see what principles you can draw from there.

Leader's Note

Distribute the "Ministry of Defense" handout and divide into groups of 3-4. Give them 10-12 minutes to work on these, then pull the groups back together to discuss their responses. Note that there are many principles they could come up with. Go with what they give you. As always, the responses we include here are not "the right answers," but just suggestions.

Gideon starts out full of questions about the way God works.
Possible Principle: We all have questions and doubts. That won't keep you from serving God.

Gideon thinks he is unworthy to act on God's behalf.
Possible Principle: When we feel unable to stand up for God, he has us exactly where he wants us.

Gideon is told to reduce the size of his army, so God will get the credit.
Possible Principle: "Not by might, nor by power, but by my Spirit, says the Lord Almighty" (Zechariah 4:6). He will not accomplish his work through our brilliant debating or our dazzling style, but only by our trust in his power.

After the victory, Gideon sets up a memento of his own faith, and people worship it.
NOTE: This was the strange story of the golden ephod. Since it was a priestly garment, and Gideon set it up in his home town, we're assuming it was like a statue to honor Gideon's own righteousness.
Possible Principle: It's not about how good a Christian you are. It's always about God.

Read 1 Peter 2:11-12.
Possible Principle: Practice what you preach. If you're talking about how God can fill a person's life, let him fill yours.

Read 1 Peter 3:15-17.
Possible Principle: Be prepared. Answer with "gentleness and respect."

Read 1 Peter 5:6-9.
Possible Principle: Be humble and trusting. Watch out for the devil, but don't be anxious.

Just Do It

What is your "Ministry of Defense"? As you go through your life each day, where do you need to step up and speak out? Is there are a particular friend who challenges you to defend your faith? Is there a particular teacher? Is there a class where these questions come up, or is it just in conversations that arise in the cafeteria.

At the bottom of your handout, I want you to write down a name, a place, or a time – anything that would define your "Ministry of Defense." If the angel of the Lord appeared next to you at school and said, "I want you to step up *here*," where would that be?

Then look back over the principles you jotted down. We've learned lots of things from Gideon and Peter, but what is one thing you need to pay special attention to, as you step up for Christ with this person, or in this place? Circle that principle, and ask God for help in applying it.

11 men from mars

Objectives

- Group members will learn how Paul defended the Christian faith in secular environments.
- They will learn how to speak about their faith in their own world.

Bible Reference

Acts 14:1-6; Acts 17.

Preparation

Go to www.BlueFishTV.com/Handouts and click Revolution Volume 1. Then click on the *Men from Mars* lesson to download "*Just in Case*" handout and make copies for the whole class; pens or pencils.

Startup

What's your favorite color? Of all the colors in the spectrum, which do you think is best?

Leader's Note

Ask several people, getting several different colors.

Why is that your favorite color? What makes that color better than the others?

Well, you can't all be right, can you? If red is the best color, then all you green-lovers are just plain wrong. If green is the best color, then you'd better start convincing everyone who said blue.

Leader's Note *This is supposed to be fun, so have fun with it. Carry it as far as it will go.*

What's wrong with this whole approach? Why can't we all agree on the best color?
(It's personal preference. There's no right or wrong, just opinions.)

In our world today, people tend to treat your religion like your favorite color. There's no real right or wrong, they say. It's a matter of personal preference. So for you to try to convert someone else to your religion is like trying to talk them into adopting your favorite color.

What's 2 + 2? What's 6 x 7? What's the square root of 81? What year was the Declaration of Independence signed? Who wrote the play *Hamlet*? What two elements make up table salt? (4; 42; 9; 1776; Shakespeare; sodium and chlorine.)

Defend your answers. Why do you say 2 + 2 = 4? Why do you say Shakespeare wrote *Hamlet*? (It's just true. These are facts.)

I've asked two types of questions here. First we had the matters of preference. "What's your favorite color?" And then we had matters of fact – two plus two.

How about these questions? "Is there a Creator? Was Jesus the Son of God? Did he rise from the dead"?

Most people today say it's all a matter of preference. And it's true that many believers worship the kind of God they prefer. But are there any facts involved? Is there any right or wrong to it? Can we prove that certain beliefs are valid and others aren't?

As we look at the full picture of religious belief, we find both types of questions. There are many matters of preference in religion. Some prefer to worship God with a lot of music or candles or incense, while others prefer a simple style. Some see God as a righteous judge while others emphasize his merciful forgiveness. But at the heart of our faith there are certain statements that are either true or they aren't.

- Was the universe created by God?
- Was Jesus the son of God?
- Did Jesus rise from the dead?
- Does God affect people's lives today?

These are "2 + 2" questions. If I say yes and you say no, one of us is wrong. We can't both be right. Now I can love and respect those who disagree with me, but I can't say it doesn't matter. If I like yellow and you like purple, we can hold our different opinions and it doesn't really matter. But if I believe Jesus is the Son of God and my neighbor doesn't, then it does matter. By the laws of logic, one of us is mistaken. And that may have eternal results.

Bible Discovery

We'll come back to those questions in a little bit. But first we should take a look at how the apostle Paul tried to convince others about Jesus. Turn to Acts 14. Would someone read the first verse?

When they entered a city like Iconium, where did Paul and Barnabas usually start preaching? (The synagogue.)

This is where Jews worship. They went because they were Jewish, and because Christianity is based in the Jewish faith. Jesus came as the Jewish Messiah, who would offer salvation to the whole world.

As a result of their preaching, who believed in Jesus? ("Great numbers of Jews and Gentiles.")

It might be surprising that Gentiles (non-Jews) were also at the synagogue, but throughout the Roman Empire, a number of Gentiles became interested in the laws and traditions of Jewish faith. These folks were called "God-fearers" or "God-worshipers" because they honored the God of the Jews even though they weren't Jewish.

When Paul came around, preaching that Jesus was the Messiah for Jews and Gentiles alike, these God-fearers would be very excited. It was like they were being welcomed into the family. Some of the Jews also trusted in Jesus as their Messiah. But other Jews opposed the radical message Paul was preaching. Would someone read verse 2?

Who was causing problems here? ("The Jews who refused to believe.")

This became the pattern wherever Paul traveled. When he arrived in a city, he first preached at the synagogue. Some synagogues were very receptive and they'd let him preach regularly. But eventually there would be conflict between those who accepted Jesus and those who didn't. Paul would be asked to leave – sometimes forcibly.

In Iconium, people were talking about stoning Paul and Barnabas to death, so they skipped town. But in other, less violent cities Paul would simply move down the street and find a public place to preach that would be even more welcoming to Gentiles. A church would form there, made up of both Gentiles and believing Jews.

Turn to Acts 17. Paul is now visiting Thessalonica with a new partner, Silas. As usual, he goes to the synagogue first. Would someone read verses 2-4?

So Paul speaks in the synagogue services for three weeks, and what is the content of his message? (That the Messiah had to die and rise from the dead, and that Jesus was the Messiah.)

When he said that "Jesus . . . is the Christ," what did he mean? (Christ is the Greek term for the Hebrew word Messiah. Both words mean "anointed one." Throughout the Old Testament there were promises of a leader who would come, specially empowered by God to save his people. This was the Messiah, or the Christ.)

What resource material was Paul using? (The Scriptures. The Old Testament.)

In the Jewish synagogue, they would be very familiar with the Old Testament Scriptures. That was their Bible. Paul was a trained rabbi so he knew this stuff backward and forward. He would quote prophecies about the Messiah – probably including Isaiah 53, where it talks about the Anointed One as a servant who was "wounded for our transgressions." He might talk about the Messiah as the Passover Lamb, whose blood protected the people from judgment.

So first he was talking with the people about what they were looking for. *This is the Messiah God promised to send you!* And then he talked about how Jesus fit that profile. Born of a virgin, as prophesied. Born in Bethlehem, but preaching in Galilee, as prophesied. Bringing sight to the blind and freedom from demons, as prophesied. Betrayed by a friend and put to death like a criminal, as prophesied. And just as David had prophesied that the Holy One could not stay dead (Psalms 16:10), so Jesus rose from the dead. This is your Messiah, Paul said. Jesus is the one you're looking for!

According to verse 4, who responded to his message? (Same as before. Some Jews and a large number of God-fearers.)

Take a look at verse 5. What happens . . . again? (Trouble. Some unbelieving Jews start a riot to oppose Paul's preaching.)

Leader's Note *In various parts of Scripture it talks about "the Jews" opposing Jesus or his message. Obviously it doesn't mean all Jews, since we were just told that some of the Jews believed Paul's message. In this case it refers to a group of violent Jews who fought against what Paul was preaching.*

As this chapter goes on, we find Paul and his team escaping to another town, but then trouble arises, so Paul slips out to Athens and waits there while his associates, Silas and Timothy, wrap up business in the last town. But this isn't any vacation for Paul. It's a new opportunity. Would someone read Acts 17:16-17?

What was Paul "distressed" about? (The city was full of idols.)

It says he was "reasoning," or debating. Where did he do this? (In the synagogue, as usual, but also in the marketplace.)

Four or five hundred years earlier, great philosophers like Socrates, Aristotle and Plato came from Athens, and the city was very proud of that heritage. In fact, they seemed to have a sort of "Philosophy Club" that met regularly on one of the hills in Athens. They took their name from that hill – Areopagus (AIR-ee-OPP-uh-gus), sometimes known as Mars Hill. The place was named for the god of war, Ares (or the Roman Mars), but these guys were doing battle with their brains. A few of these philosophers heard Paul talking in the marketplace. Let's see what happened. Someone read verses 18-21.

What was their initial reaction to Paul and his ideas? (He was a "babbler." These were "strange ideas." But they wanted to hear more.)

So Paul is asked to defend his faith in front of the Philosophy Club. How would you feel if you had to do that? How would you prepare? (It would be nerve-wracking. Maybe you'd want to read a lot of philosophy or carefully spell out every point in outline form. Or maybe just pray a lot.)

Somebody read verses 22-23.

What does he say about the people of Athens? (They're very religious.)

Remember that he was "greatly distressed" about all the idols he saw. So why does he compliment them on being "very religious"? (He wants them to hear the rest of what he has to say. He doesn't want to alienate them from the start.)

What altar does he make special reference to? (The one with the inscription "TO AN UNKNOWN GOD.")

Scholars have various ideas on why there is an alter inscribed "to an unknown God." One theory suggests that there was a disaster that the city was spared from. They weren't sure which of their gods saved them, so they put up this altar to say, "Whoever you are, thanks." Or it might just be that they didn't want to leave anyone out, in case they had forgotten some deity.

As we read through his message in Athens, we'll find that he does not quote Scripture at all. Why not? (They don't know Scripture. They don't believe it. It wouldn't mean anything to them.)

Look down at verse 28. What *is* his source material? (He quotes some of the local Greek poets.)

When does he start talking about Jesus? (Right at the end. In verse 31, he mentions "the man God has appointed" and he talks about the resurrection.)

Let's review.

When Paul spoke to the Jews, he used *their* source material, the Scriptures. When he talked to Gentiles, he used their source material – their idols and their pop songs. With the Jews he started by talking about *what they were looking for*. They expected a Messiah, and Paul looked through Scripture with them to figure out what the Messiah would have to be like. Essentially, he did the same thing in Athens. He talked with the philosophers about *what they were looking for*. Yes, there were lots of idols in town, but he zeroed in on the altar TO THE UNKNOWN GOD. He figured out that they were looking for a God who could not be boxed up in an idol or temple, someone who could fill their lives and have a relationship with them. In both cases, with Jews and Greeks, Paul said, "Jesus is what you're looking for!"

So What?

As you think about your classmates, your friends and neighbors, the ones who don't know Jesus, what do you think they're looking for?

Leader's Note *This is a hard question, so it might take a minute before they respond, but it's very important. Wait for them. People might be looking for fun, escape, or sex. But they might also long for significance, something interesting, or steadfast love.*

Remember that Paul walked around the city looking at the idols. Maybe you need to do some "walking around" and ask people what they're looking for. Who is the "Unknown God" in our culture?

Let's talk about source material. If you're trying to witness to someone, should you say, "Believe in Jesus because the Bible says he's the Son of God"? (It depends on whether they believe the Bible, and many people today don't. What is the trusted source material of your hearers?)

Please understand this. The Bible is the trusted source material for *your* life, and it should be. *You* believe it's God's Word to humanity, but many of your classmates don't. So if you're trying to convince them to look into Jesus, start with *their* source material. Eventually you will share the story of Jesus from the Bible, explaining how he fulfills what they're looking for.

Leader's Note *Distribute the "Just in Case" handout.*

In our world today there are many with a kind of "scientific" mindset. Faith doesn't come easy. They want to prove everything. And sometimes they assume that Christianity is all about turning off your brain and just believing in some fairy tale. That's not the case, but that's what they think.

Here's an info sheet. It doesn't explain everything, but it might spark some additional research on your part. Take a moment right now to go through and put a star next to any point that really makes sense to you. If there's something you don't get, put a question mark beside it. If there's something you want to share with someone in your world, circle it.

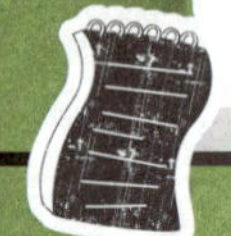

Leader's Note *There's not room or time to go in-depth on all these points. Feel free to do your own research. Just go through the points to make sure the group has a basic understanding of them. A few extra comments are included here in parentheses.*

The Case for Creation

Premise: It makes sense to believe that the universe was created by God.

• **Science can trace things back toward the beginning, but there must be a First Cause.** (This is a classic Proof-of-God argument. You can keep asking, "Where did that come from?" but eventually you reach a First Cause.)

• **Science generally accepts a single explosive moment at the beginning – the big bang. It is reasonable to believe that God was responsible for that initial explosion.** (Some Christians don't accept the big bang theory; that's fine. But isn't it possible that the big bang was the way God chose to kick things off?)

• **Some organisms are irreducibly complex, meaning that they could not have developed through natural selection. This suggests some sort of intelligent design.** (The classic work here is *Darwin's Black Box* by Michael Behe. A cellular biologist, Behe suggests that cells are like mousetraps, with several distinct parts that work together to survive. Individually, these parts would not improve survival skills, so they could not have evolved separately. They must have been put together by an intelligent force.)

• **Science properly explores the processes of the natural world, and it theorizes natural explanations for how things came to be. But it oversteps its own authority when it asserts that there can be nothing supernatural.** (Most Christians are not anti-science. But we want science to do science and stay away from religious pronouncements. When scientists claim that their theories "prove" that there is no Creator, that's a religious pronouncement, and it's bad science.)

The Case for Jesus

Premise: There is good evidence to believe that Jesus of Nazareth is divine.

• **Focus on the resurrection. If Jesus rose from the dead, that proves that he was more than just a man.** (We just saw this in Acts 17:31. The apostles frequently stated that Jesus' resurrection was the main proof of his divinity.)

• **A body disappeared from a guarded, sealed tomb. Jesus' enemies, both Roman and Jewish leaders, would have every reason to produce the body, if they could.** (Josh McDowell makes this point well in *Evidence that Demands a Verdict*. The empty tomb is a strong testimony to the resurrection.)

• **Jesus' followers seemed more surprised than anyone. They claimed that Jesus not only rose but appeared to them, ate with them and talked with them.** (Some people buy a "spiritual" resurrection, where somehow Jesus' ideas got reborn within his followers. But they reported several physical encounters with him.)

• **Many of his closest followers died rather than renounce their belief in the risen Lord.** (This may be the strongest testimony. If the resurrection was a hoax, would the eyewitnesses die for it?)

• **Look at the quality of Jesus' teachings. This is brilliant stuff, and yet Jesus spoke of his own divinity as well.** (Many are drawn to Jesus by the power of his teachings, but he said many bold things about himself as well, such as "I and my Father are one." C.S. Lewis makes this point well in *Mere Christianity*. If Jesus isn't Lord, he's a liar or a lunatic – but you can't call him just a great teacher.)

• **Look at the prophecies. For centuries before Jesus, Jewish prophets were talking about a coming Savior. Jesus fulfilled those prophecies.** (This goes way beyond proof-texts. The whole sacrifice was set up with Jesus as its culmination. Abraham's faith, Moses' law, and David's dynasty were all fulfilled in Jesus.)

• **Look at what happened to the Christian movement after Jesus left. Persecuted for 250 years by the greatest empire on earth, Christianity still emerged as the major religion of that empire.** (Christians were opposed first by their fellow Jews. As the movement spread towards Rome, the Roman Empire unleashed its fury, beginning with Nero in 64 AD and continuing through Diocletian in the early 300s. Persecution wasn't non-stop, but it came on a regular basis. The historical emergence of Christianity does not prove its validity, but it does cry out for an explanation. Could it be that truth won out, and the power of God was seen in these suffering saints?)

The Case for Faith

- **We can prove that it is reasonable to believe in a Creator, and we can say it's logical to believe in Jesus as the Son of God, but it still comes down to a commitment of faith.**

- **So what are you looking for in life?**

- **Looking for love? Jesus died to prove his love for you. The church is full of people committed to expressing that love.**

- **Looking for significance? Jesus has work for you to do, and he will empower you to do it. Each Christian becomes a servant to others.**

- **Looking for an escape from boredom? Jesus is the most amazing person you will ever know.**

- **Looking for a new start? In Christ you are a new creature. He died to forgive you.**

- **There are many good reasons to trust in Jesus, but one philosopher has suggested there's no good reason *not* to. If it's false and you believe it, no big deal. But if it's true and you don't – then you're really missing out.** (This is another classic argument, Pascal's Wager.)

Just Do It

Where is your "Areopagus?" Where is your Mars Hill? Where do you need to stand up and speak about your faith? At school? Hanging out with friends? In a chat room?

And what will you say? Notice that Paul didn't scold the Athenians for worshiping idols, even though that bothered him. Instead he said, "I'm glad you are seeking for God. Let me tell you where to find what you're looking for." And before he did any of that, he learned about the state of their souls before he said a word. "Be ready to give an answer for the hope you have," the Bible tells us. How will you get ready?

NOTE: You may want to do some additional research yourself, or suggest books to your students.

Evidence that Demands a Verdict, by Josh McDowell (and other McDowell books)
The Case for Christ, by Lee Strobel (and other Case books by Strobel)
Mere Christianity, by C.S. Lewis
How Now Shall We Live, by Charles Colson and Nancy Pearcy (look for other Pearcy books, too)
Darwin's Black Box, by Michael Behe (scientifically heavy)
My Truth, Your Truth, Whose Truth? by Randy Petersen

12 impact

Objectives

- In the video, group members will see examples of young people changing the world by serving the Lord.
- In the video and lesson, they will be challenged to consider the impact they could have on the world around them.

Bible Reference

Acts 1:8; 1 Timothy 4:12.

Preparation

Go to www.BlueFishTV.com/Handouts and click Revolution Volume 1. Then click on the *Impact* lesson to download "*Gut Check*" handout and make copies for the whole class; set up TV/DVD player; *Impact* DVD; pens/pencils; chalkboard or equivalent; globe or world map.

Startup

Can you give me an example of a Christian who has changed the world?

How has that person changed the world? What difference did he or she make?

What talents or characteristics did that person have that God used in this world-changing process?

Leader's Note

You might get people saying, "Jesus" or "Paul," and that's fine. But try to steer them to modern times. Then you might get people choosing political leaders, which is fine, but don't get sidetracked into a political argument.

Let's bring it closer to home. Can you give me an example of a Christian who has changed this town? *[Or county, region, or state, depending on your geography.]*

What difference have they made? What abilities did God use?

Can you give me an example of a Christian who has changed your school?

How? What did they do?

As we'll see today, there are lots of ways to change the world. God may use you to share his love with millions, or he might have a task for you right here in this town, or in your school. The question is not whether you'll get famous, but whether you'll be faithful in serving the Lord. We'll see some great examples of faithfulness in today's video.

Showtime

Show *Impact* video

Re:view

Of the different stories and interviews in the video, which was your favorite and why? Shane and Shane? The Sudan ministry? Helping Hearts in the homeless shelter? Passion Magazine?

Did any of them inspire you to do something similar? How do you think you could make that happen? (Some ministries require special education, but others don't. Just by talking it up, you could probably get a church ministry started for homeless shelters or other charitable work in your region. And any kid with a computer can start a Christian blog or website.)

In your Bibles, turn to Acts 1:8. It's after the resurrection. Jesus has been teaching his disciples for forty days, and now he's about to go back to heaven. Somebody read verse 8.

Jesus said his disciples would be "witnesses." What does it mean to be a "witness"? (To tell someone what you have seen or experienced.)

Jesus said that to them, but it also applies to us. We should share with others what we have experienced with Jesus. How do we do this? By talking with them, certainly, by telling them the good news. But in the video, Doug Fields made an interesting comment. "When Jesus said, 'You will be my witnesses,' he didn't mean just be my witnesses *verbally*. One of the ways to be a witness . . . is to go meet somebody's *physical* needs."

What do you think about that? Do you agree? (This falls in line with many other Bible verses, where Jesus blesses the one who "gives a cup of cold water" in his name (Matthew 10:42); where he challenges us to meet the needs of "the least of these, my brothers" (Matthew 25:40); where he says that we will be known by our "fruits," that is, our actions (John 15:5); and "By this will everyone know that you are my disciples, if you have love for one another." (John 13:35))

You know, this was true in history. For most of the first three centuries after Jesus, Christianity was an underground movement. The Romans made it an illegal religion and sometimes hunted down Christians and killed them. But somehow, Christians also became known for their love. If you were a Roman and your child was sick, and if you were too poor to see a doctor, you might send word to the Christians, and they might come and nurse your child back to health. This was the kind of love that eventually won over the Roman Empire.

Do you think meeting physical needs like hunger or homelessness is more important than telling people about Jesus? (Of course not, but they need to go together. It's not either/or. It's both the verbal good news of Jesus and his love in action.)

Do you know what a mission agency is? Sometimes they're called mission boards or mission societies. These are companies that exist for the purpose of finding missionaries, equipping them, helping them raise funds, and sending them out to tell people about Jesus and to share his love in many ways. Some send missionaries around the world, while others focus on this country, or particular types of local ministry.

What if we were a mission agency? What if this class decided to find ways to meet various needs around the world and close to home? I'm not saying we have to do this, but . . . *what if?*

What parts of the world could we help? Is there a particular country or group of people you feel especially concerned about?

Are there particular needs in our town, region or state that we could find ways to meet?

Leader's Note

Write their ideas on a board, if you have it. If you've brought a globe or world map, identify the places they mention. If the group doesn't come up with suggestions of their own, you could list some examples from the video and include some ministries your own church supports.

We'll come back to this list, but I want to ask you about some other ideas in the video. At the start, Shane and Shane were talking about being "gifted" with their music ministry. They said that God's "gifting" comes to other people in other ways. What does "gifting" mean? (They were *not* saying, "Hey, look at us! We're so gifted!" They were saying that God gives different abilities to different people. We all need to use whatever abilities God has gifted us with.)

Toward the end of the video, Doug Fields said: "God is the great chemist who says, 'Let's take the needs of the world and the talents of the people and put them together.' But now you've got to come alongside of him and figure out what you love to do and discover where you're gifted."

In one beaker are the needs of the world. In another test tube are the gifts he has given to us. He puts them together – leading us into certain areas of ministry, finding needs that match our gifts. So maybe Sudan is not the right place for you, but another place is. Maybe you really shouldn't be doing ministry to the homeless, but you should be doing something else.

So, how do you find the right place for you to minister? (Pray. Talk with wise people who know you. Get to know your own abilities. Become familiar with a wide range of needs and ministries.)

Just Do It

Leader's Note

Divide into groups of 4-5. If close friends want to be in the same group, this time that's great. Distribute the "Gut Check" handout. Give them 6-8 minutes to work through it.

Each one of you should fill out the worksheet for yourself, but ask the others in your group for help. They may have ideas about the kind of person you are, as well as the type of ministry you could do.

[After 6-8 minutes]

You've probably got a lot of different ideas bubbling right now. Is there anything you'd like to share with the group?

Did any of you come up with an idea for a group project we could all get involved with?

Leader's Note

Your time is limited now, but make plans to follow up soon with any workable ideas. Your class really could do something.

As we close, I'd like you to turn to 1 Timothy 4:12. The truth is you really can make a difference. And that's not just my thinking. It's in the Bible. Somebody read 1 Timothy 4:12.

Objectives

- Group members will explore biblical teaching about helping others in need.
- They will think about how they can demonstrate their faith and change the world by doing the deeds that please God.

Bible Reference

Luke 10:30-37; Ephesians 2:8-10; Hebrews 10:23-25; chapter 11 (especially v. 6); James 2:14-17; 1 John 3:17-18.

Preparation

Go to www.BlueFishTV.com/Handouts and click Revolution Volume 1. Then click on the *Sam I Am* lesson to download "*What the World Needs Now*" handout and make copies for the whole class; pens or pencils; (optional) box of props.

Startup

Do you know the story of the Good Samaritan? Let's review it.

Leader's Note

Ask them what they know. Fill in missing details as needed.

- A guy is traveling and he gets attacked by bandits.
- While he's lying by the side of the road, two different religious leaders pass by without helping him.
- A third passerby stops to help him. This man is a Samaritan, a member of a hated race and religion.
- Still, he helps the wounded man, taking him to an inn and paying for his care.

We're going to divide into groups of five or six, and I want each group to act out the story of the Good Samaritan in some modern way. You can make the Samaritan a Goth or a groupie. You can make the passersby into politicians or prom queens. Just make sure you get the basic points of the story. If you want to consult the original, you'll find it in Luke 10:30-37.

[*Optional*] Oh, and to make it even more fun, each group must use at least one prop from this box.

Leader's Note *The prop option could be a fun one. Gather a box full of odd items – toys and hula hoops and caulking guns and funny hats, etc. Give the groups 6-8 minutes to develop their stories, then have the presentations.*

[*After the presentations*]

Which of these versions did the best job of getting the point across? Why?

What is the point of the Good Samaritan? (That's a tough question. On the surface it seems that it's a challenge to do good, to help people in need. And that is one lesson we can learn here. But Jesus told the story in answer to a specific question: "Who is my neighbor?" It would have shocked people that the hero of this story was a hated Samaritan. So the deeper lesson is something like: *Reach across social boundaries to give and receive help. That's what it means to truly "love your neighbor."*)

Bible Discovery

Turn to James 2:14. Would somebody read that verse?

What's the answer to that question? Can you be saved by a faith like that, a faith that has no deeds?

We need to understand this very carefully, because the New Testament says several things about faith and good deeds. We have to get the whole picture. So let's read on a little. Would somebody read James 2:15-17?

James writes a little skit for us, with two characters. Who are they? (A needy person and a person with "faith" who extends warm wishes.)

In this scene, the needy person is freezing and starving. What does the other person do about that? (Nothing, really. The person says, "God bless you," sort of, but doesn't really help.)

What point is James trying to make? (True faith has to go beyond words. You can't just say "Be warm and well fed." You need to act. You need to provide warmth and food.)

In verse 17, what does James call faith without deeds? (Dead.)

In what way is it dead? (It does no good. In the case of the freezing, starving person, that kind of faith makes no difference. It provides nice words, but no action.)

So let's get back to our first question. Are we saved by the good works that we do?

The answer is still no. We are saved by faith alone, but true faith results in good deeds. Yet it might be good to let the students mull this over for a while and discover it for themselves.

We'll come back to James 2, but let's take a detour into Ephesians 2. Would someone read Ephesians 2:8-9?

According to these verses, what saves us? (Grace, through faith.)

What's the difference between grace and faith? (Grace is what God gives us, his kindness that we don't deserve. Faith is our way of receiving it.)

You might think of it this way. You walk into a room and you flick a switch and the light comes on. What makes the light shine? You might think that you made it shine by flicking the switch, but it's really the electricity providing the power. Your switch-flicking merely allowed the electricity to come through. It's the same way with grace and faith. God's grace makes it happen; our faith merely allows the grace to flow.

According to Ephesians 2:8-9, what does NOT save us? (Our works. We do not earn the grace of God. In that case, it wouldn't be grace. It would be payment.)

Somebody read verse 10.

According to this verse, what should our purpose in life be? (Good works.)

There's a little pun in this verse. We are God's "good work," and he wants us to do good works. In fact, he has created us for that very purpose.

So, what have we learned from Ephesians 2 about faith and good works? Do good works save us? Are good works important for us to do? (Verse 9 says explicitly that our deeds do not save us. We cannot earn God's grace; it is a gift. We can merely receive it in faith. But *then* God works within us, prompting us to do the good works he wants. So, yes, works are important, but they follow after our salvation. They don't save us.)

Let's turn back to James 2, picking it up in verse 17. Somebody read verses 17-18.

What relationship do you see here between faith and deeds (or good works)? (Faith needs to be accompanied by action. If not, it is a dead, useless faith. We demonstrate our faith by our deeds.)

Does this contradict Ephesians 2? (No, not really, but it does give us a new spin. The overall teaching of Scripture is that works do not save us, but they do prove that faith is genuine.)

Leader's Note *By the way, there have been a number of scholars through the centuries – including Martin Luther – who had difficulty putting together these two passages. So if your students are struggling with it, they're in good company.*

For the moment, let's replace the word *faith* with the word *love*. Imagine that you're starting a new romance. When you talk on the phone, your new boyfriend or girlfriend says, "Oh, I love you so much!" So you say, "Let's get together on Friday after school," and they say no, they can't make it. Saturday? No, they have to be somewhere. You go through the whole week, and then another week, and there's always some excuse. On the phone they say, "I love you I love you I love you," but they don't do anything about it.

Would you say that's a good relationship? Why? (The words are there, but not the actions. Love requires time and dedication. You might wonder if there's really any love there.)

It's the same way with faith. You can say the words of faith, but if there's no commitment, maybe it's not really faith. Somebody read James 2:19.

What is he saying here? (It's good to believe in God, but that's nothing special, since even demons believe there's a God.)

What's the difference between the way you believe in God and the way demons believe in God? (Demons do the acts of evil. Presumably, we let our faith in God motivate us to do good things.)

So maybe there are two kinds of faith. Maybe there's a kind of mental belief that God exists – this is the basic belief that even demons have. And then there's *believing in* God, or *trusting in* God – and that means committing our lives to him. It's faith from the heart, which is confirmed when we do the actions that God likes.

Glance over the rest of James 2. There are two examples of people whose faith led them into good works. Who are they? (Abraham and Rahab.)

What did Abraham do? (Among other faithful actions in his life, he obediently took his only son to be sacrificed. At the last moment, God spared the son.)

What did Rahab do? (She protected the Israelite spies in her home.)

These people didn't just say, "Oh, God is cool." They did some difficult and dangerous things because of their commitment to the God they believed in.

Flip over to the previous book, Hebrews. In chapter 11, we find all sorts of examples of faith in action. I'm going to give you a few minutes to skim through Hebrews 11 and find one example that you find especially interesting.

Who is it, and what did they do?

Leader's Note *If they need more direction, make specific suggestions: Abel in verse 4, Enoch in 5, Noah in 7, Abraham in 8, 11, or 17, Isaac (20), Jacob (21), Joseph (22), Moses (23, 24, or 27), the Israelites (29,30), Rahab (31), or the various figures of 32-38.*

So is this chapter saying that you have to do some kind of heroic act in order to be saved? (No! It is saying that the obedient actions of these Old Testament people came out of their faith.)

Their faith in God gave them a sense of what was important, and that affected the decisions they made. They saw the world around them, and it wasn't just about getting rich or having fun. Through faith, they knew that there was a God who made that world, and so the most important thing was to love God and do what he wanted. Faith led them to do the right thing. Let's go back to verse 6, tucked away in the middle there. Would someone read Hebrews 11:6?

What do we need to have to please God? (Faith.)

This verse defines faith in two ways. What are they? (Believing, first, *that he exists* and, second, *that he rewards those who earnestly seek him.*)

How do you think he rewards those who earnestly seek him? (Well, what do those people want? What are they looking for? Him! So he rewards their search by revealing himself to them, by being there for them, by entering into a relationship with them.)

Thinking back to what James said, what kind of faith do even the demons have? (The first kind. They believe that God exists.)

So, according to Hebrews 11:6, what additional faith do we need to have in order to please God? (The second kind. The faith that believes it's worthwhile to seek God, and so you do seek him.)

We're not just playing word games here. Throughout the New Testament we're told about a *relationship* with God that changes everything for us. We don't just believe that he's out there somewhere. We earnestly seek a relationship with him. The Bible tells us that our sin has kept us away from God, but Jesus forgave our sin through his death on the cross, so now God can offer us this amazing relationship with him. We can't earn it by being good; we just receive it by faith, believing that he will be there for us.

Once we enter that relationship, the transformation begins. Through his Spirit, God empowers us to do the good things he has always wanted us to do. Not that we're perfect. We still make some big mistakes along the way, but he keeps molding us, shaping us, making us more like him. That's because our faith is alive, it's real, it's active, it's part of an ongoing relationship.

James tells us that some people have a dead faith, and you can tell because they're not doing good stuff. They may believe that God exists out there somewhere. And they might even accept some facts about Jesus dying on the cross. They believe as much as demons believe, but they've never entered that relationship with God. They believe that God is "out there," but not "in here." You might call that faith, but James says it's a useless faith.

Leader's Note

Take this next step as the Spirit leads you.

[Maybe some of you have that first kind of faith, but not the second. You've been doing the church thing, so you know the facts about God and Jesus. But there's nothing alive about your faith, because you've never opened up to that relationship. God wants you to seek him. And if you do, he will reward you by entering your life in a big way. He will give you fulfillment and joy and power. He will transform you.

Is that what you want? Then tell him. Maybe this is a time when you can talk to God in a new way. Say something like this: "God, I've always believed you were out there, but now I want you in here. Jesus, I always knew that you died for our sins, but now I know it's my sin that you want to forgive. I want a relationship with you. I want you to be there for me. I want you to transform me. In Jesus' name. Amen."

If you just prayed that prayer, please talk with me later. I'd love to know about it, so I can pray for you as God starts doing his thing in your heart.]

So What?

We've been talking about faith and good deeds. I hope you've gotten the point that it's not an either-or thing. The two go together. A living faith transforms us, and that leads us to do good things. But we're not alone in this. As Christians we help each other. Flip back to Hebrews 10:23-25. Would someone read those verses?

There's lots of "let us" in this salad. (Sorry!) What are the things that we should "let ourselves" do? (Hold unswervingly to our hope. Spur one another on. Not give up meeting together. Encourage one another.)

These people were living in a time when it was tough to be a Christian. They looked forward to "the Day" when Jesus would return. As they faced persecution and opposition, it would be easy to give up hope, but not if they encouraged one another.

I'm especially interested in verse 24. What's the result of "spurring one another on"? (Love and good deeds.)

How can we "spur one another on to love and good deeds"? (By pointing out needs that we could meet. By reminding one another of God's love and challenging one another to show it to others. By applauding one another when we do something right, especially when it's a difficult choice.)

A spur is a pointed thing that pokes an animal so it moves forward. Spurs hurt. If you're a horse, and your rider kicks a spur into your side – *ouch!* It's not a gaping wound, but it smarts a little. In the same way, maybe we need to sharply challenge one another to do what needs to be done. Turn to 1 John 3:17-18. We may see some spurring going on right here. Would someone read those verses?

What picture is John painting? (A rich Christian next to a needy person, but the rich Christian isn't helping.)

What's wrong with this picture? (If a Christian has God's love within, then he or she will help the needy.)

According to verse 18, how should we love and how should we NOT love? (Not just with words, but with actions.)

Isn't this just what James was saying? It's not enough to say, "God bless you! Be warm and well-fed." We are called to action – feeding and clothing the needy.

Leader's Note

Distribute the "What the World Needs Now" handout.

John talks about "seeing your brother in need." It starts with the seeing, so let's brainstorm that a bit. You see a grid here, including three different types of needs you might find in four different environments.

What might be included in physical needs? (Hunger, health issues, homelessness, poverty, etc.)

What might be included in emotional needs? (Loneliness, depression, getting picked on, various addictions, a need for love and acceptance, etc.)

What might be included in spiritual needs? (The need to know God, to trust Jesus, to hear about Jesus, to know how to pray, etc.)

Before we break into groups, I want you to spend a couple of minutes thinking about your friends and family. You don't have to fill in every space on this chart, but use it to think through the different types of needs that people have. Think about the physical, emotional, and spiritual needs of your friends at school and in the neighborhood. Then think about your family – what needs do you see there?

Write down the names and needs that come to mind. If there are private matters you want to keep private, you could use code names or initials.

Leader's Note

After about 2 minutes of individual work, break into groups of 5-6. Give them 8-10 minutes to work together.

In your groups, I want you to brainstorm the other areas of this chart. What needs do you see in the community or in the world?

[*About halfway through their work time*] If you haven't already, move on to the questions at the bottom. Choose one of the needs you've listed, and think about how this class could do something about it. Then pick another need and do the same thing.

[*With a few minutes left*] You should be wrapping that up and moving to the last two questions. Take some quiet time individually to think about what you could do individually to meet a need. Then ask the others for help. What can they do to encourage you, challenge you, or spur you on?

[*Pulling them all back together*] What did you come up with? Did you find any ways that this class could address some needs in the community and the world? Let's hear them.

Just Do It

Leader's Note *Focus on one project that everyone seems to like. Break it down into steps. If you're raising money for famine relief, how do you start? The first step might be gathering info about the need, the second might be sharing that info with the church or community. Use your adult wisdom to foresee pitfalls, get the appropriate church approvals, etc. If this activity has to be continued next week, or in a midweek planning meeting, great! Just be sure to get some specific steps in mind.*

Before we go, I want to remind you about those bottom two questions. We may be excited about what this group can do, but what will you do individually to meet a need that you see?

And how will your little group of five or six help one another to meet those needs? Will you pray for that person, e-mail a reminder, get the report later? We can make a big difference in our world if we just spur one another on to love and good deeds.